Compiled by
Restaurant Recipes

*These recipes were submitted by some of the
Arkansas Ozarks best known restaurants as
well as some great places off the beaten-path.
The one thing they have in common is they
are all mouth-watering dishes that you can
prepare in your own kitchen. Enjoy!*

Special Thanks from the Publisher:
This cookbook would not have been possible without the support of all the restaurant owners, chefs and sponsors who appear in this book.

Copyright © 2006 Restaurant Recipes

Library of Congress Control Number: 2006907196

ISBN-10: 0-9778057-1-9

ISBN-13: 978-0-9778057-1-6

First Edition, Second Print

Printed in Canada

Published by:
Recipe Publishers
A division of JEC Publishing Co.
2049 E. Cherry Street
Springfield, Missouri 65802

Toll Free (800) 313-5121
www.recipepubs.com
www.jecpubco.com

Publisher: JE Cornwell
Senior Advisor: Judith Cornwell
Graphics Design: Tom Dease
Project Advisors: Jim Martin

Contents

The Best of the Arkansas Ozarks

4

RESTAURANT

Recipes of

APPETIZERS & BEVERAGES

BOSTON MOUNTAIN GRILLE

3251 N. College
Fayetteville, AR 72703
(479) 443-9299

You can see, smell and taste the pride every time you come to Boston Mountain Grille because we have partnered with local businesses to help serve you the very best food from the Boston Mountains. Quality deli meats from Ozark Mountain Smokehouse, fresh baked rolls from Stone Mill Bakery and our signature "Coca Cola Cake" from Rick's Bakery.

Razorback Layer Dip

6 oz. cream cheese
12 oz. black beans

12 oz. Rotel
6 oz. cheddar cheese

Directions

Take 6 oz. cream cheese and press firmly in the bottom of an oven safe dish. After mixing the Rotel and black beans together with even parts and draining all juices. Spread evenly over the layer of cream cheese. Cover the Rotel and beans with shredded milk cheddar cheese.

Preheat oven to 300° and bake dish for 30 minutes or when all cheese is melted.

Submitted by Doug Mantan, owner

COOL WATER STEAKS • SEAFOOD • PUB

STEAKS•SEAFOOD•PUB

2217 N. College Ave.
Fayetteville, AR 72701
(479) 571-3636
www.coolwatercafe.com

Cool Water Cafe features an eclectic mix of thick-cut OMAHA steaks, fresh seafood, tasty pastas, signature sandwiches, crisp salads and tempting desserts served by the friendliest people. Open for lunch and dinner 7 days a week plus our famous Sunday Brunch. For business lunches, a special dinner or a family outing, you can't beat the atmosphere or the value. And our private banquet room comfortably seats 100, perfect for receptions, parties or conferences.

Focaccia "Pizza"

1- 3"x6" square of fresh herbed Italian flat bread of choice (pre-cooked).
3 Tbsp. fresh pesto of choice.
1 oz. fresh blanched Julianne sun dried tomatoes
2 oz. fresh mozzarella provolone blend cheese.
1 tsp. freshly grated Parmesan cheese.
2 fresh Julianne basil leaves
1 oz. of heavy cream
Extra virgin olive oil, salt & pepper to taste.

Directions

Spread out evenly 2 of the 3 Tbsp. of the pesto onto the flat bread. Top with sun dried tomatoes than the mozzarella and provolone blend. Drizzle with the olive oil and sprinkle with salt and pepper. Bake at 350 ° until golden brown.

While baking combine the rest of the pesto and cream in a small sauce pan bring to simmer than remove from heat. Spread out on a small serving dish. Place pizza on top of sauce garnish with Parmesan and basil leaves.

Submitted by Michael Obersteadt, chef

COOL WATER STEAKS • SEAFOOD • PUB

2217 N. College Ave.
Fayetteville, AR 72701
(479) 571-3636
www.coolwatercafe.com

Cool Water Cafe features an eclectic mix of thick-cut OMAHA steaks, fresh seafood, tasty pastas, signature sandwiches, crisp salads and tempting desserts served by the friendliest people. Open for lunch and dinner 7 days a week plus our famous Sunday Brunch. For business lunches, a special dinner or a family outing, you can't beat the atmosphere or the value. And our private banquet room comfortably seats 100, perfect for receptions, parties or conferences.

Jelly Bean

1½ oz. vanilla rum
Pineapple juice
Grenadine

1½ oz. mango rum
Orange juice

Fill a cocktail glass with ice. Add rums. Fill almost to top with pineapple juice. Top with a splash of orange juice and grenadine.

Pooty Tang

2 parts Absolut Mandarin vodka
1 part Grand Marnier

1 part Red Bull
2 parts orange juice

Shake all ingredients with ice. Strain into a glass. May be served as a shooter or a cocktail.

Hemingway Breeze

2 oz. light rum
2 oz. pineapple juice

2 oz. cranberry juice

Serve in a highball glass over ice. Garnish with an orange slice.

Seven Seas Sunset

1 oz. light rum
1 oz. Malibu coconut rum
Grenadine
Pineapple juice

1 oz. Myer's Dark Rum
Barcardi 151
Orange juice

Fill large cocktail glass with ice. Pour in grenadine until bottom of glass is covered. Add light rum, dark rum, and coconut rum. Fill glass halfway with orange juice. Fill to top with pineapple juice. Top with a splash of 151. Garnish.

Submitted by Justin Luther & Autumn Parker

DINO'S ITALIAN RESTAURANT

4628 Hwy. 62 East
Mountain Home, AR 72653
(870) 492-5080
dinositaliancuisine.com

In 1993 we opened Dino's Italian Restaurant in beautiful Mountain Home. The restaurant has a very relaxing atmosphere, soft music and decorated in fine Italian art. Great selection of fine dishes, wines, beers and desserts.

Scampi Dino

Cook fettuccine in salted boiling water (al dente)

7 big shrimp	4 Tbsp. white wine
2 Tbsp. butter	Pinch of real Saffron
1 c. whipping cream	1 tsp. minced garlic
4 oz. Parmesan cheese	Salt and pepper

Directions

Marinate the Saffron in 4 Tbsp. of warm white wine, add cream, garlic and let boil for 1 minute. Reduce heat, add Parmesan, mixing well for a minute or two. Salt and white pepper to taste. Sauté shrimp in 2 Tbsp. butter for 2 minutes on each side. Add shrimp to Saffron cream sauce. Served over fettuccine.

Submitted by Eliana and Dino, chefs and owners

EMELIA'S MEDITERRANEAN KITCHEN

309 W. Dickson St.
Fayetteville, AR 72701
(429) 527-9800

Emelia's Kitchen is named for the owner's mother. We use Armenian recipes that George grew up on and learned from Emelia. We use only the finest vegetables, meats and fish. We also do brunch on Saturday and Sunday mornings.

Tropical Sunrise

½ oz. Mt. Gay Vanilla Rum   ½ oz. Mtgay Mango Rum
Any fruit mix of juices you prefer. Mine is
peach, orange mango juice with a splash
of grenadine.

Directions

Fill tall glass with ice. Combine rums then fill with juice leaving room to finish with splash of grenadine. Garnish with slice of orange and a cherry.

Submitted by Sara Lusher, owner

FOREST HILL RESTAURANT

Hwy. 62 E.
Next to Holiday Inn
Eureka Springs, AR 72632
(479) 253-2422
www.foresthillrestaurant.com

Opened in 1996 and located in historic Eureka Springs, AR, Forest Hill has always prided itself on pleasing the customer. With a variety of foods to choose from including choice steaks, an excellent buffet or wood burning oven pizzas, we have everything to fulfill your every need. We also have homemade desserts prepared in our own bakery! Be sure to drop by for a satisfying and enjoyable dining experience.

Spinach/Artichoke Dip

9 oz. cooked, chopped spinach
½ lb. cream cheese
½ c. diced black olives
¼ c. chopped parsley
1 Tbsp. salt
1 Tbsp. garlic powder

9 oz. chopped artichoke hearts
½ c. minced red onion
¼ c. diced pimento
4 c. shredded Parmesan cheese
1 Tbsp. pepper

Directions

Combine spinach and artichoke hearts. Blend with red onion, black olives, pimento, parsley and Parmesan cheese. Add salt, pepper and garlic powder to make a wonderful dip for any occasion. Serves. 8.

Submitted by Pat Alexander, chef

JOSE'S MEXICAN RESTAURANT

324 W. Dickson St.
Fayetteville, AR
(479) 521-0194
www.oleforjoses.com

The famous historic Jose's, a long standing landmark, is located in the heart of the entertainment district, Dickson Street, in Fayetteville, AR. The driving force of Jose's Mexican Restaurant & Cantina for the last 25 years still exists. Jose's offers world famous margaritas and salsa made fresh daily with the finest ingredients. The concept is simple–great food, great service, great fun. Ole for Jose's!

Party Cheese Dip

2 Tbsp. plus 2 tsp. butter
2 Tbsp. plus 2 tsp. garlic, chopped
3¼ c. heavy cream
2½ lbs. white cheese, grated
1 tsp. white pepper
½ tsp. cayenne pepper

¼ c. diced onion
¼ c. flour
3¼ c. milk
¼ c. jalapeno peppers, chopped
1 tsp. cumin
½ tsp. hot chili powder

Directions

Saute onions and garlic in butter until soft. Add flour and cook for one minute. Add milk and cream. Bring to a boil. Turn the heat down to low and add cheese slowly, stirring constantly until cheese is melted. Turn the heat down to low and add cheese slowly, stirring constantly until cheese is melted. Turn the heat off and add jalapeno peppers and remaining spices.

Submitted by Neal Crawford, owner

JOSIE'S STEAKHOUSE

50 Riverbank Dr.
Batesville, AR 72501
(870) 793-7000

Josie's Steakhouse began as an addition to a dairy bar and gas station in Waldenburg, AR in 2001. Named after the first granddaughter of proprietors Steve and Beth Carpenter, Josie's quickly became famous for providing the highest quality food in a fun, family focused atmosphere. In February of 2004, the Carpenter family brought their homemade flavor and down-home flair to Batesville, opening at the beautiful Lockhouse Restaurant overlooking the White River. Priding itself on providing the highest quality food possible, Josie's is one of only a few restaurants in Arkansas that serves hand-carved 100% Certified Angus Beef steaks, one of the highest quality meats on the market. From karaoke contests and out door dining to event catering and live concerts, Josie's aims to please by providing the place where good times are had, memories are made and everyone feels at home!

Fresh Salsa

1 gal. diced tomatoes with juice
6 sprigs fresh cilantro
1½ c. red onions, chopped
1 Tbsp. garlic
1 can green chili peppers
1 Tbsp. garlic pepper seasoning

½ c. lime juice
1 bell pepper
½ c. green onions, chopped
2 Tbsp. cumin
½ c. jalapeno
1 Tbsp. salt

Directions

Blend everything together, add cilantro last. Be careful not to add too much.

Submitted by David Sours, chef

OZARK MOUNTAIN SMOKE HOUSE

Farmington, AR 72730
(800) 643-3437

In 1946 a small smokehouse was built by Roy Sharp and the Ozark Mountain Smoke House was launched as a business/hobby(?). In 1962 Roy's son, Frank, and his wife, Sara, became actively involved in the business, which they still operate (with their four children) on the Sharp farm on the slopes of Mount Kessler. Visitors are cordially invited to visit Mount Kessler and the smokehouse and kitchens of the Ozark Mountain Family.

Salami Stacks

2 (3 oz.) pkgs. cream cheese
1 tsp. chopped parsley
1 lb. smoked salami, thinly sliced

2 tsp. prepared horseradish, drained
2 Tbsp. grated onion

Directions

Combine cream cheese, horseradish, parsley and onion. Mix well. For each "cylinder" spread 7 slices of salami with cream cheese mixture, stacking them to form a cylinder. Top with a slice of sausage. Repeat for each cylinder. Wrap in waxed paper and chill for 3 hours or more. When ready to serve, cut each stack into 6 or 8 wedges. Yield: 7 "cylinders" or 42-56 wedges.

Smoked Turkey Savory Spread

Directions

Mix well 1 cup finely ground smoked turkey, ½ cup soft butter, ¼ tsp. Tabasco. Serve on crackers or toasted bread rounds.

Smoked Turkey Rolls

Directions

Split 6 finger rolls in half horizontally and scoop out the soft centers, leaving the crust and reserving the bread crumbs. Moisten the crumbs with two tablespoons hot milk and combine with ¼ cup each of grated cheddar and minced smoked turkey. Stuff the roll crusts with the mixture. Reassemble the rolls, arrange on baking sheets and brush the tops with melted butter. Bake in slow oven for about 15 minutes, until they are slightly toasted and the cheese is melted.

Submitted by Ozark Mountain Family Cookbook

PARK PLACE GRILL

At The Clarion Hotel
1255 S. Shiloh Dr.
Fayetteville, AR 72701
(479) 521-1166

BY CHOICE HOTELS

Park Place Grill inside the Fayetteville Clarion Inn offers a friendly dining experience. A taste of the South can be found within our Daily Breakfast Buffet or our Traditional Lunch Buffet. Dine by candlelight from a complete dinner menu featuring a variety of appetizers and entrees. Or, just stop n to try our famous Clarion Burger. We hope to see you at our Friday Night Seafood & Prime Rib Buffet or join us for Sunday Brunch, both are Traditions since 1986!

Clarion Stuffed Mushrooms

3 lbs. cream cheese, softened

Finely dice:
1 med. red onion
4 green onions

2 ribs celery
2 lbs. pulled crab meat

Combine all of the above and mix well.

Add:
6 drops dry sherry
1 tsp. cayenne pepper

1 tsp. white pepper
¼ tsp. nutmeg

Mix well by hand and chill. When stiff, roll into approximately ¾ Tbsp. balls and stuff into mushroom caps. Top with Parmesan cheese and paprika. Broil until browned.

Submitted by Jerry Conell, executive chef

POWERHOUSE SEAFOOD & GRILL

112 N. University
Fayetteville, AR 72701
(479) 442-8300

A former electric power company from the early 1900s, Powerhouse Seafood offers a unique and entertaining casual atmosphere that has been award-winning since the doors were reopened in 1992. With private banquet rooms, outside live entertainment and a large variety of menu options with daily dinner and drink specials, Powerhouse Seafood can take care of all of your dining needs.

Parmesan Spinach Dip

2 boxes spinach, chopped
1 c. chopped onion
3 c. mayonnaise
1 Tbsp. Italian seasoning
1 tsp. black pepper

5 c. Parmesan cheese, grated
12 oz. cream cheese
1 Tbsp. Louisiana hot sauce
2 tsp. garlic powder
7 oz. dried water chestnuts

Directions

Rinse and drain the spinach. Combine all ingredients and mix very well. Spread on garlic bagel chips and place in a moderate oven until warmed throughout.

Submitted by Cortney Richardson, prep cook

POWERHOUSE SEAFOOD & GRILL

112 N. University
Fayetteville, AR 72701
(479) 442-8300

A former electric power company from the early 1900s, Powerhouse Seafood offers a unique and entertaining casual atmosphere that has been award-winning since the doors were reopened in 1992. With private banquet rooms, outside live entertainment and a large variety of menu options with daily dinner and drink specials, Powerhouse Seafood can take care of all of your dining needs.

Mike & Marty

A concoction made famous by two great Powerhouse friends. This warm dessert-style coffee is great after any meal, anytime of year.

½ oz. Frangelico
½ oz. Baileys
Whipped cream
Coffee

½ oz. Kahlua
½ oz. creme de cacao (white)
Chocolate syrup

Pour Frangelico, Kahlua, Baileys, creme de cacao (white) into Irish coffee glass. Fill with coffee and top with whipped cream followed by chocolate syrup on top.

Cajun Mary

Made with a variety of spices, this spicy cocktail complements any meal at Powerhouse Seafood, especially if you'd like to spice it up with one of their Cajun entrées.

1½ oz. Absolut Peppar Vodka
¼ bar spoon of horse radish
3 dashes pepper
Jalapeno slice
Pimento stuffed olive
Bloody Mary mix

3 dash Louisiana hot sauce
3 dashes granulated garlic
3 dashes gumbo file
Celery stalk
Blackening seasoning
Lime slice

Combine Absolut Peppar, Bloody Mary mix, hot sauce, horse radish, garlic, pepper and gumbo file in a shaker. Add ice and shake vigorously. Pour into a drinking glass rimmed with blackening seasoning. Garnish with the celery stalk, lime slice, jalapeno slice and pimento stuffed olive.

Submitted by Doug Tomlinson, bar manager

ST. JAMES WINERY

540 Sidney St.
St. James, MO 65559
(800) 280-9463
www.StJamesWinery.com

St. James Winery is owned and operated by the Hofherr Family since 1970, conveniently located on Interstate 44, on Old Historic Route 66 only ninety miles southwest of St. Louis, Missouri in St. James, Missouri .

With over 700 miles of vines in Missouri, Arkansas, and Michigan, no other winery in the Eastern United states utilizes such state of the art technology from the vineyards to the bottling room bringing you consistent quality vintages for your enjoyment. With over 1,800 medals to date, no wonder St. James Winery is "America's Midwest Winery". In our area, be sure to stop by our tasting room and sample our wide variety of vintages, our extensive gift shop, and take a tour of our cellars. St. James Winery products are presently distributed in six states and available on our website.

Fondue a'la St. James

1 c. St. James Winery Vintner's Select Seyval
6 oz. Swiss cheese, shredded
2 Tbsp. flour

6 ounces Gruyere cheese, shredded
⅛ tsp. ground black pepper

Directions

In a medium bowl toss cheeses with the flour until evenly mixed. In a 2-quart saucepan, heat wine over medium high heat until very hot but NOT boiling.

Reduce heat to medium low. Add one handful of the cheese mixture to the wine; stir constantly and vigorously until the cheese melts and the mixture is thick and smooth. Repeat with remaining cheese mixture. Stir in pepper.

Serve immediately or in a heated fondue pot with your favorite bread and vegetables.

Submitted by Jack Bonar

RESTAURANT *Recipes of* SOUPS & SALADS

178 CLUB RESTAURANT

2109 Central Blvd.
Bull Shoals, AR 72618
(870) 445-4949
www.178club.com

We pride ourselves in maintaining the highest standard of quality and excellence so common fifty years ago, but so rare today. We are family owned and operated and are proud to have been at this same location in Bull Shoals for over 26 years. We prepare your meal when you place your order, using only the highest quality and freshest ingredients to ensure your dining pleasure. You see, we are not resting on a reputation; we're building one!

Mountain Cabbage Soup

½ lb. ground beef
1 c. diced potatoes
1 c. sliced carrots
3 Tbsp. butter
1½ c. beef broth

4 c. or one small head of shredded green cabbage
½ c. chopped onions
1 Tbsp. flour
1½ c. prepared Hidden Valley Ranch Buttermilk Orig. recipe ranch salad dressing

Directions

Brown ground beef in large sauce pan. Drain. Add cabbage, potatoes, carrots and onion. Cook and stir in butter. Cook until potatoes are tender but not brown, about 5 minutes. Stir in flour and then add in the remaining ingredients. Simmer about 20 minutes. Makes about 6-8 servings.

Submitted by the Fox family

BALCONY RESTAURANT & BAR

12 Spring Street
Eureka Springs, AR
(479) 253-7837

Come to the Basin's Balcony Restaurant for lunch or dinner, overlooking downtown Eureka Springs – a historical vacation getaway in Arkansas. On weekends we feature great live music preformed by local musicians while you relax in the fresh mountain air. True culinary delights await you in the historic ambiance of the Basin Park Hotel. Our mission: "What we serve our guests is not just a meal ordered but a pleasant memory hand-crafted by well-trained and caring culinary professionals." Come Join Us!

Broccoli Cheese Soup

3 qts. heavy cream
½ gal. whole milk
3 lbs. American cheese (sliced or cubed)
¼ c. cavenders seasoning

1 qt. half 'n half
2½ lbs. sour cream
2 c. shredded Colby/Monterrey Jack blend
3 lbs. fresh broccoli

Directions

Heat all liquids to just before boiling point. Add cavenders, then American cheese gradually stirring well in between additions until all cheese is incorporated. Add sour cream and shredded cheese, stir well.

Cut broccoli into bite-sized pieces and steam until al dente. Remove liquids from heat and add broccoli. Makes approximately 3 gallons.

Submitted by Penny Gentry

BALCONY RESTAURANT & BAR

12 Spring Street
Eureka Springs, AR
(479) 253-7837

Come to the Basin's Balcony Restaurant for lunch or dinner, overlooking downtown Eureka Springs – a historical vacation getaway in Arkansas. On weekends we feature great live music preformed by local musicians while you relax in the fresh mountain air. True culinary delights await you in the historic ambiance of the Basin Park Hotel. Our mission: "What we serve our guests is not just a meal ordered but a pleasant memory hand-crafted by well-trained and caring culinary professionals." Come Join Us!

Chicken Paradise Salad

5 lbs. cooked chicken breast, fine diced
1 - 20 oz. can crushed pineapple
10 green onions, chopped
2 c. mayonnaise
½ c. chopped walnuts

1 lb. red grapes, cut in half
1 bunch of celery, fine diced
1 tsp. Louisiana hot sauce
½ c. brown deli mustard
Cavenders seasoning to taste

Directions

Prepare and mix all ingredients. Serve on croissant or bed of lettuce as a salad.

Submitted by Penny Gentry

BLUFF STEAKHOUSE AT BIGGER'S BED & BREAKFAST

Overlooking the Spring River

20 Bluff Rd.
Hardy, AR 72542
(870) 856-4718
www.biggersbnb.com

At Bigger's Bed & Breakfast Bluff Steakhouse we create a homey atmosphere with casual fine dining. Our customers are our best advertisers. If you're looking for great food – look no further.

Pea and Ham Soup

1 small pkg. split peas	1 onion, chopped
1 carrot, grated	3 garlic cloves, chopped
1 tsp. sea salt	Ground pepper to taste
1 c. ham, diced	4 c. water
2 Tbsp. olive oil	1 tsp. granulated garlic w/parsley
2 c. rye, white and wheat bread	1 Tsp. olive oil

Directions

Combine peas, water and ham. Bring to a boil. Reduce heat and cook for 45 minutes covered. Stir often. Sauté onions, garlic in olive oil. Add to pea mixture. Just before serving add grated carrots, salt, pepper and granulated garlic w/parsley.

Herbed croutons: mix rye, white and wheat bread. Sprinkle with olive oil and garlic salt w/parsley. Broil and watch closely. Stir often. Sprinkle on top of soup.

Submitted by Valerie Bathrick, owner

BRENDA'S SALE BARN CAFE

706 Townsend Dr.
Pocahontas, AR 72455
(870) 892-0240

This recipe is a town favorite. Brenda's has an all-u-can-eat buffet Monday thru Friday, 11 a.m. to 2 p.m., featuring southern cooking at its best. Buffet includes salad bar and dessert. Saturday features an all-u-can-eat breakfast buffet. Brenda's hours are Mon.-Fri. 6 a.m. - 2 p.m.; Sat. Breakfast Only – 6 a.m. - 11 a.m. Cattle sale is Tuesday at 1:30 p.m. Cafe is open until 8 p.m. on Tuesdays only.

Best Macaroni Salad in Town

8 c. macaroni
1 c. celery, chopped
1 c. onion, chopped
½ c. pimento, drained
1 c. cheese, shredded
1 c. green pepper, chopped

5-6 c. salad dressing
1 c. sugar
1 Tbsp. Worcestershire sauce
1 Tbsp. cider vinegar
1 Tbsp. celery seed
Salt and pepper to taste

Directions

Cook macaroni as directed. While cooking macaroni, in a large bowl mix salad dressing, sugar, Worcestershire sauce, vinegar and celery seed. Stir until sugar is dissolved. Drain macaroni and cool with cold running water (drain) add rest of ingredients except cheese and macaroni. Mix well and chill. Before serving add cheese. Makes about 10 quarts. Salt and pepper to taste. Add tuna or chicken for a main dish.

Submitted by Fern, Patty and Brenda

CHELSEA'S CAFE

10 Mountain St
Eureka Springs, AR 72632
(479) 253-6723

Slightly OFF Center at Mountain: Great Food Prepared Fresh Daily! Ice Cold Beer, Wine and Mixed Drinks! Live Music Inside, or on our Enclosed Patio! The Friendliest Locals in Town! Chelsea's Corner Café has been in business for 17 years. We are a local hangout And have built our reputation on catering to Locals, Live Music and Dancing. We are the place where all the misfits - fit and we love to entertain the tourist!

Tortilla Soup

4 grilled chicken breasts
3 qts. water
2 c. diced tomatoes
2 Tbsp. cumin
Salt to taste

Chicken stock, 49 oz. can
2 lbs. roasted green chiles
2 large red onions
½ c. minced garlic

Directions

Bring broth and water to a boil, add chicken and cook for 7 minutes. Turn to simmer and add tomatoes, onions and green chiles. Add cumin, garlic and salt to taste. Cook for 20 minutes. Turn off and add cilantro.

Serve with a handful of corn chips and cheddar cheese.

Submitted by Vicky "Stick" Brown

COOL WATER STEAKS • SEAFOOD • PUB

2217 N. College Ave.
Fayetteville, AR 72701
(479) 571-3636
www.coolwatercafe.com

Cool Water Cafe features an eclectic mix of thick-cut OMAHA steaks, fresh seafood, tasty pastas, signature sandwiches, crisp salads and tempting desserts served by the friendliest people. Open for lunch and dinner 7 days a week plus our famous Sunday Brunch. For business lunches, a special dinner or a family outing, you can't beat the atmosphere or the value. And our private banquet room comfortably seats 100, perfect for receptions, parties or conferences.

Apple Chicken Salad

2 c. fresh spring mix greens
½ red apple, seeded and sliced
3 Tbsp. bleu cheese dressing
1 tsp. sliced green onion

1 - 6 oz. chicken breast
6-8 red seedless grapes
1 Tbsp. honey
Pinch of black pepper

Directions

Season and grill chicken breast. Whisk together bleu cheese dressing, honey and green onions. Toss greens with dressing and place in a large bowl. Top with sliced chicken, grapes and apple slices.

Submitted by Michael Obersteadt, chef

ELLA'S RESTAURANT AT THE INN AT CARNALL

465 N. Arkansas Ave.
Fayetteville, AR 72701
(479) 521-0401

Located at the historic Inn at Carnall Hall on the corner of the University of Arkansas' beautiful campus, Ella's Restaurant offers exquisite fine dining with a pinch of history. The cuisine features classic French procedures with modern French style. We use only local produce brought in daily and the highest quality meats and fish available. Open for breakfast, lunch, and dinner Monday-Saturday, as well as for Sunday brunch. Come experience something better.

This salad is irresistible during the summer. Use only very fresh tomatoes from a farmer's market if available. At the restaurant we use a French bleu cheese, Roquefort, but any soft bleu will work. For optimal results, allow cheese to sit out for a few hours, as cheese is best served closer to room temperature.

Bleu Cheese in Tomato, Basil & Arugula Salad
With Bacon and Bacon Vinaigrette

For Salad:

8 grape or cherry tomatoes, halved
1 Roma tomato, diced
½ packed basil, thinly sliced
½ c. cooked chopped bacon, reserved from dressing (see below)
Bacon Vinaigrette (see below)

1 Roma tomato, sliced
2 c. baby arugula
½ c. bleu cheese, softened

Directions

Place all ingredients in mixing bowl and add a good amount of dressing. Toss to coat. Serve on a plate with bleu cheese crumbled on top of salad. Garnish with fresh basil leaves.

For Vinaigrette:

8 grape or cherry tomatoes, halved
1 Roma tomato, diced
½ packed basil, thinly sliced
½ c. cooked chopped bacon, reserved from dressing (see below)
Bacon Vinaigrette (see below)

1 Roma tomato, sliced
2 c. baby arugula
½ c. bleu cheese, softened

Directions

In a blender combine all ingredients except oil, salt, and pepper. Pulse until combined. On high speed slowly add oil in a continuous stream until fully emulsified. Salt and pepper to taste.

Makes two main course servings or four first course servings

Submitted by Travis D. Maier, executive culinary artist,
and Aaron Nix, assistant culinary artist

EMELIA'S MEDITERRANEAN KITCHEN

309 W. Dickson St.
Fayetteville, AR 72701
(429) 527-9800

Emelia's Kitchen is a healthy favorite for those watching their weight or just loving fresh light foods. Emelias serves a variety of kebobs and fish. We also do the Mediterranean appetizers that you would expect...humus, baba knosh, tabouli and stuffed grape leaves.

Spinach Salad

Small bag of baby spinach
2 hard boiled eggs, sliced
1 Roma tomato, sliced
2 oz. feta cheese
Add garlic, salt and pepper to taste

¼ c. of diced walnuts
¼ c. of Greek olives
Dressing, virgin olive oil
Splash of lemon juice

Directions

In a small salad bowl mix greens, feta cheese, olives and walnuts with dressing (premixed). Top with tomato and hard boiled eggs. Use any garnish you like, parsley, crushed red peppers, etc.

Submitted by Sara Lusher, owner

FRED'S HICKORY INN

"Keeping the Tradition Alive"
1502 N. Walton Blvd.
Bentonville, AR 72712
(479) 273-3303

Fred's Hickory Inn was started with the idea that "if we can serve quality food, offer good service and provide a comfortable atmosphere people will dine with us." Thirty-six years later we still slow smoke our meats on Fred's Original Smoker. We use the best quality meat available. Our steaks and chops are hand cut and grilled to perfection. And, of course, our spaghetti and cheesecake are Miss Lou's original recipe.

Sherry and the staff at Fred's are committed to keep the tradition that our founders and friends, Fred and Lou Gaye, started in 1970 alive for future generations.

Sherry's Tomato Onion Salad

4 sliced tomatoes
1 c. red wine vinegar
2 Tbsp. sugar
1 Tbsp. chopped up fresh basil
Dash of white pepper
1 c. of feta or blue cheese for garnish

2 large Vidalia onions
½ c. olive oil
1 tsp. ea. oregano, rosemary, thyme
½ tsp. salt
Salad greens your choice

Directions

Slice tomatoes and onions in a glass bowl. Put dressing ingredients in a jar. Shake and pour over tomatoes and onions. Let marinate overnight. Place on bed of salad greens of your choice and top with cheese.

Submitted by Sherry Mendenhall, owner

INDIAN HILLS COUNTRY CLUB

337 Snead Dr.
Fairfield Bay, AR 72078
(501) 884-6001

Indian Hills Country Club is nestled in the lush rolling hills of Fairfield Bay, Arkansas. You can relax and dine in rustic comfort or you can romp and chow down at our many special events. Southern service with a smile, as you indulge your appetites in the atmosphere of your choice, for a real fine dining experience, or a casual meal and cocktail in our 19th hole. Bring the whole family and explore our lake, golf courses and many other amenities.

Bistro Salads

½ + ¼ c. shredded cheese, divided.
  (we currently use Parmesan)
4 or 5 oz. shrimp, steak, chicken or fish
1 tsp. minced garlic

1 or 2 c. loosely packed salad greens
  (we like baby greens)
2 tsp. oil (we use olive oil)
Cherry tomatoes and black olives (opt.)

Directions

Using a 6" to 10" nonstick heated skillet, sprinkle ½ c. shredded cheese thinly. Cook until it slightly begins to bubble and become golden. Nearby, have an inverted glass or bowl to determine the shape and size of the toasted cheese bowl you desire. Using a heat resistant spatula, begin to loosen the edges of cheese crisp in skillet. Remove from heat and invert onto glass or bowl.

While cheese crisp is molding, heat oil in skillet and add meat of your choice and garlic, cooking to desired doneness. While meat is sautéing, fill your crispy cheese bowl with salad greens, top with cooked meat and sprinkle with remaining cheese. Cherry tomato and black olive garnish is optional.

Serve with dressing of your choice. Balsamic vinaigrette is a current particular favorite here.

Submitted by Bonnie M. Todd, kitchen manager

JOE'S BISTRO

3061 N. College Ave,
Fiesta Square
Fayetteville, AR 72703
(479) 443-5637
www.eatatjoesbistro.com

Joe's Bistro serves original French-Italian cuisine. The restaurants menu is about three years in the making. It is composed mainly of experiments in cooking for friends that turned out "better than expected." Joe's also boasts a full bar, catering services and a banquet room that holds about 20 people. Students receive 25% off their entrees with ID.

Boiled Shrimp Salad with Lime Sour Cream Sauce

Salad:

½ c. diced red bell peppers or roasted red bellpeppers
½ c. diced avocado
¼ c. chopped fresh cilantro
1 or 2 chopped fresh jalapeno (optional)
1 Tbsp. extra virgin olive oil
½ lb. peeled and deveined shrimp

½ c. diced Roma tomatoes
½ c. chopped fresh spinach
¼ c. chopped green onions
1 Tbsp. chopped fresh garlic
2 Tbsp. red wine vinegar
Juice of ½ lemon and ½ lime
Salt and pepper to taste

Directions

Place shrimp in a pot of cold water and bring to a boil, cover and remove from heat. Let the shrimp stand for 3 or 4 minutes, then place in ice water to cool. Roughly chop shrimp, and combine all ingredients in a large mixing bowl. Mix well and add salt and pepper to taste. Place in refrigerator for at least an hour (the longer the better). Serve cold over baked tortillas and top with a dollop of the lime sour cream.

Sour Cream Sauce

2 c. sour cream
Juice of 1½ limes

2 tsp. chopped lime zest
Salt to taste

Combine ingredients in a bowl mix and refrigerate

Submitted by Joe & Jennifer Utsch, owners

THE LAKEHOUSE RESTAURANT

2809 Hwy. 101
Gamaliel, AR 72537
(870) 467-5250

Nestled in the Ozarks overlooking Lake Norfork in Mt. Home, Arkansas. The Lakehouse Restaurant & Lounge has been serving USDA Choice Steaks and Prime Rib since 1994. Other menu items include grilled chicken, seafood, appetizers, and out of this world homemade cheesecake! Kids menu. Open Tue-Sat at 4:00 p.m.

Cheesy Potato Soup

8-10 Baked potatoes
2 c. all-purpose flour
2 c. sliced scallions
1 gallon milk
1 c. bacon bits

1 lb. Margarine
Salt & pepper to taste
1 c. sour cream
2 c. shredded cheddar cheese

Directions

Melt margarine, add flour, salt & pepper to make a rue, add milk. When it starts to boil and thicken, add the cheese, scallions, bacon bits and sour cream. Add potatoes, stir and enjoy!

Submitted by Trish Beck, owner

LOAFIN JOE'S

201 West Mountain Street
Fayetteville, AR 72701
(479) 443-9944
www.loafinjoes.com

The original Loafin Joe's is located one block south of the Square in downtown Fayetteville on the corner of Church and Mountain Street. The original founder and owner, Joe Weber, has a new location as well in Springdale off 40th Street on Elm Springs Road.

Loafin Joe's serves hot sub sandwiches, served on made-from-scratch bread, homemade potato chips, BIG salads, and pizza too. All our menu items are made with the highest quality meats, cheese and fresh vegetables. Open for lunch and dinner Monday through Sunday with the best Happy Hour in town! Come see why we're not your ordinary, average, everyday Joe!

Aunt Susie's Salad

1 lb. baby spinach leaves
1 pt. of sliced strawberries
Fresh bacon bits
For Dressing (in a blender, put):
  1 c. of sugar
  2 Tbsp. of poppy seeds
  ½ tsp. paprika

1 c. of fresh bean sprouts
1 can of sliced water chestnuts

4 Tbsp. of sesame seeds
½ tsp. Worcershire sauce
½ c. cider vinegar

Directions

Start blending ingredients. While blending, slowly add ½ c. of oil Blend until thick. Put on salad before serving and toss.

Submitted by Joe and Jennifer Weber, owners

MEADOW STREET BAR & GRILLE

70 N. E. Avenue
Fayetteville, AR
(479) 442-5555

Meadow Street Bar & Grille is located on the second floor of the Radisson Hotel. We are conveniently located on the downtown square in beautiful downtown Fayetteville.

Lobster, Mango and Avocado Salad
With Chile-Lime Vinaigrette

1¾ lb. live lobster, ½ ea.
¼ ea. mango, peeled
Dressing:
   2¼ tsp. olive oil
   ¾ tsp. jalapeno, minced
   ¾ tsp. lime zest

½ ea. avocados cut in ½" pieces
1 c. watercress and parsley

2¼ tsp. lime juice
¾ tsp. honey

Directions

Bring a large pot of salted water to a boil. Drop lobster head first into water, cover and cook 6 minutes. Remove and cool. Remove meat from shell. Whisk oil and next 4 ingredients in bowl, season with salt and pepper, cover and chill. Rewhisk dressing before serving. Slice avocados and mango and fan on plate. Spoon some dressing over lobster and season with salt and pepper. toss greens in another bowl with remaining dressing. Place greens on plate, place lobster on top of greens and serve.

Submitted by Dave Wilson, chef

MYRTIE MAE'S

207 W. Van Buren
Eureka Springs, AR 72632
(479) 253-9758
www.myrtiemaes.com

It was in the 1920's. A widow, Myrtie Mae struggles to support her children renting cabins and serving meals to her guests. A sign tacked to a tree promises her famous Fried Chicken dinner and homemade pies. Today, Myrtie Mae's is located at Best Western Inn of the Ozarks and still serves the best Ozark Fried Chicken, the freshest Salad Bar and home made specials every day.

Strawberry Soup

15 oz frozen sliced strawberries,
   thawed, with juice
3 oz. sifted powdered sugar
1 oz. half and half

15 oz. sour cream
1 oz. vanilla extract
½ oz. grenadine syrup
1 oz. heavy whipping cream

Directions

In a mixer, mix strawberries and sour cream together. Beat slowly until well mixed. Add grenadine, vanilla and sugar while mixing until mixture becomes smooth. Add half and half and cream last and stir until just blended. Chill and serve. Shake well before serving. Garnish with fresh sliced strawberry. (Serves six)

Submitted by Dave Heilemann

OZARK MOUNTAIN SMOKE HOUSE

Farmington, AR 72730
(800) 643-3437

In 1946 a small smokehouse was built by Roy Sharp and the Ozark Mountain Smoke House was launched as a business/hobby(?). In 1962 Roy's son, Frank, and his wife, Sara, became actively involved in the business, which they still operate (with their four children) on the Sharp farm on the slopes of Mount Kessler. Visitors are cordially invited to visit Mount Kessler and the smokehouse and kitchens of the Ozark Mountain Family.

Wilted Lettuce Salad

5 slices bacon
2 heads leaf lettuce or garden lettuce
   torn in bite size pieces
¼ tsp. salt
¼ c. cider vinegar

2 hard-boiled eggs, chopped
2 chopped green onions
1 Tbsp. sugar
¼ tsp. pepper
2 Tbsp. cold water

Directions

Fry bacon until crisp. Drain on paper towels. Reserve drippings. Combine lettuce, onion and chopped egg in salad bowl. Combine bacon drippings and other ingredients and heat to boiling. Pour over lettuce, toss lightly.

Note: On a scorching summer day, serve with fresh corn bread for a refreshing light supper.

Chicken Salad Supreme

2 c. finely diced smoked chicken
1½ c. finely diced celery
½ c. mayonnaise

½ c. sour cream
1 c. grated sharp cheese
¼ c. toasted almonds

Directions

Mix first four ingredients and divide among four individual ramekins. Chill until ready to serve. Sprinkle with cheese and almonds. Put under broiler until cheese is melted. Tuck greens around edge and serve.

Submitted by Ozark Mountain Family Cookbook

38

PARACHUTE INN

10 Skywatch
Walnut Ridge, AR 72476
(870) 886-5918

The Parachute Inn, located at the Walnut Ridge Regional Airport, is famous not only for their delicious food and superior service, but also for the atmosphere of dining on a retired Boeing 737 Jet, a truly unique experience. The Parachute Inn has been open for five years, and in that time has welcomed guests from 48 states and foreign countries around the world. Come and join everyone at the Parachute Inn, great food and a wonderful experience is guaranteed!

Colorful Vegetable Salad

Great colors for the holidays and keeps well in the refrigerator.

6 c. broccoli florets
2 c. cherry tomatoes, halved
1 can (6 oz.) pitted ripe olives, drained and sliced
½ c. vegetable oil

6 c. cauliflower
1 large red onion, sliced
1 envelope ranch salad dressing mix
½ c. vinegar

Directions

In a large bowl, toss the broccoli, cauliflower, tomatoes, onions, and olives. In a jar with a tight fitting lid, combing dressing mix, oil, and vinegar; shake well. Pour over salad and toss. Refrigerate for at least 3 hours. Yield: 20 servings.

Submitted by Donna Robertson, owner

PARK PLACE GRILL

At The Clarion Hotel
1255 S. Shiloh Dr.
Fayetteville, AR 72701
(479) 521-1166

BY CHOICE HOTELS

Park Place Grill inside the Fayetteville Clarion Inn offers a friendly dining experience. A taste of the South can be found within our Daily Breakfast Buffet or our Traditional Lunch Buffet. Dine by candlelight from a complete dinner menu featuring a variety of appetizers and entrees. Or, just stop n to try our famous Clarion Burger. We hope to see you at our Friday Night Seafood & Prime Rib Buffet or join us for Sunday Brunch, both are Traditions since 1986!

Clarion Chicken Tortilla Soup

2 lbs. cooked chicken breast, 1" dice
1 large red onions, 1" dice
1 - #10 can diced tomatoes and juice
1 Tbsp. black pepper and salt
2 lbs. corn tortillas, cut into strips
Lightly crushed tortilla chips

1 can Rotel
3 green bell peppers, chopped
2 Tbsp. minced garlic
4 Tbsp. cumin
Diced avocado for garnish

Directions

Combine ingredients, except tortillas, with one-half gallon water in large stock pot. Bring to a boil, reduce to simmer and cook for 30 minutes. Add strips or tortillas and simmer another 30 minutes. Stir often. To serve, pour into bowl and top with diced avocado and sprinkle with crushed chips.

Submitted by Jerry Conell, executive chef

RED APPLE INN
AND COUNTRY CLUB

1000 Country Club Road
Heber Springs, AR 72543
1-800-RED-APPLE
www.redappleinn.com

The Red Apple Inn Resort is located in the foothills of the Ozark Mountains on beautiful Greer's Ferry Lake. We offer fine dining with an assortment of steaks, seafood, and homemade dessert in our dining room overlooking the lake. The Inn was designed by a student of Frank Lloyd Wright and blends in with the natural surroundings of Eden Isle.

Tropical Salad

Salad Dressing:
- ¼ tsp. ginger, ground
- ½ c. mayonnaise
- ¼ c. lime juice
- ¼ c. Dijon mustard
- ¼ c. honey
- 1 Tbsp. sesame oil

Salad:
- Mixed greens
- Pineapple chunks
- 3 Tbsp. tomato, chopped
- 4 ea. chicken breast, marinade and grilled cut chunks
- 1 Tbsp. cilantro, leaves only
- 1 Tbsp. red onion, chopped
- 2 ea. corn tortilla, sliced

Directions

Stir ginger into Dijon mustard, mix into remaining ingredients.

Mix the greens, fruit, onion, tomato together. Chopped grilled chicken breast into chunks and add to salad. Toss with dressing. Fry the corn tortilla strips and place on top of salad (optional)

Submitted by David Smith

SMOKEY BONES BARBEQUE & GRILL

643 E. Van Asche Dr
Fayetteville AR 72703
(479) 251-7517

Resembling a rustic mountain lodge, Smokey Bones Barbeque & Grill serves award-winning barbeque and a broad variety of other American favorites. Its menu features slow-smoked Baby-Back and St. Louis-style ribs, hand-pulled pork, sliced beef brisket, choice steaks, grilled chicken and fish, fresh salads, sandwiches, Buffalo burgers and Angus burgers. Some appetizers and side offerings include Barbeque Chicken Nachos, Old-Fashioned Skillet Corn Bread with crushed pecan butter, green beans and cinnamon apples. Guests also enjoy the restaurant's signature dessert – a bag of fresh "made-to-order" hot cinnamon-sugar doughnuts served with strawberry dipping sauce.

Brunswick Stew

½ chicken, (about 1½ pounds)
⅔ lb. ground beef
¾ lb. smoked pulled pork
  (or 1 lb. ground pork, see note)
¾ c. ketchup
¾ tsp. hot sauce
1 tsp. ground black pepper
¼ c. barbecue spice
1 tbsp. of yellow mustard

6 c. water
1½ lbs. onions, diced (about 4 c.)
1 - 28-oz. can crushed tomatoes
2 - 14½-oz. cans diced tomatoes in juice
¼ c. Worcestershire sauce
1½ tsp. salt
2 Tbsp. granulated sugar
2 (15-oz.) cans cream-style corn

Directions

Cut chicken into pieces, place in a stockpot and cover with water. Bring to a boil, reduce heat, cover and simmer until chicken is tender, about 30 minutes. Remove chicken; pour stock into a bowl or large measuring cup. When chicken is cool, discard skin. Pull meat from bones; discard bones. Tear meat into small pieces. Six ounces of smoked chicken meat may be used in place of raw chicken, and water or canned broth may be substituted for stock.

In a large skillet, cook beef over medium heat until about half done. Add onions; cook until translucent, about 8 minutes. Add chicken and pulled pork; stir and cook until well mixed and heated through, about 5 minutes. Remove from heat.

Transfer the meat mixture to the stockpot. Stir in 4 cups of the reserved chicken stock. Stir in tomatoes and their juice, ketchup, yellow mustard, Worcestershire sauce, hot sauce, salt, pepper, sugar, barbecue spice and corn. Bring to a boil, then reduce heat and simmer about 1 hour, stirring occasionally, adding stock if needed.

Note: When substituting ground pork for smoked pulled pork, cook the ground pork with the beef and add ½ teaspoon of liquid smoke to the stew with the other seasonings.

Submitted by Smokey Bones team

THE STATION CAFE

111 N Main St.
Bentonville AR 72712
(479) 273-0553

The Station Cafe Inc. was established in 1997. It is a homestyle family restaurant with an extensive menu to please everyone's palate. Best known for our Black Angus Steakburgers, we also have weekly specials that range from chicken kabobs to stuffed cabbages. Voted in Reader Choice Awards - 2005 as Best Burger, Best Freedom Fry, Best Place to Eat Lunch. Your satisfaction is guaranteed at The Station Cafe Inc. We proudly serve Edy's Grand Ice Cream.

Chili (it's spicy!)

1 lb. lean ground beef
2 Tbsp. oil
¼ c. Williams Chili Seasoning
1 small can tomato sauce
1 Tbsp. black pepper

2 Tbsp. chopped garlic
8 oz. diced onions
2 c. water
1 tsp. chopped red pepper
1 tsp. salt (to taste)

Directions

Add oil and garlic to pan, sauté 2 or 3 minutes then add onion and sauté 2 minutes more. Add ground beef, crumble and stir until beef is well done. Add water, salt, red and black pepper, simmer approx 2 minutes. Add Williams Chili Seasoning and mix in tomato sauce. Simmer slowly, approx 10 minutes. Mix well, stirring often. If too thick add water.

Submitted by Cecil Turner, owner

1400 Central Blvd.
Bull Shoals, AR 72619
(870) 445-4414

The Village Wheel Restaurant, located in beautiful Bull Shoals, AR has been family-owned for 24 years, serving breakfast, lunch and dinner 7 days a week. Owners Cindy Crosslin and Danette Stubenfoll opened a gift shop in March 2005 which has unique gifts for that hard-to-buy-for person. The Village Wheel Restaurant specializes in Broasted Chicken. Monday nights is all you can eat chicken. Wednesday nights feature Canadian Walleye, Thursday nights feature quail, Friday nights has all you can eat popcorn shrimp or Alaskan white fish and Saturday nights offer prime rib. Skillet breakfasts have also been added to the menu. There is a private dining room for banquets and regular customers enjoy our birthday and anniversary club.

Broccoli & Cauliflower Salad

1 bag broccoli, cut up
1-2 large red onions
½ celery
Mayonnaise to consistency
Touch of mustard

1 bag cauliflower, cut up
2-3 green peppers
Salt and pepper to taste
Sugar (to taste)

Directions

Mix all ingredients.

Submitted by Cindy & Danette, owners

WHITE RIVER CAFE

702 Highway 56
Calico Rock, AR 72519
(870)297-3999
www.whiterivercafe.com

White River Café, nestled in the foothills of the Ozark Mountains in Calico Rock, Arkansas, caters to a unique local community and the many anglers searching for the perfect trout on the nationally known White River. Established in 1972, and still family owned and operated, the Café is known for its "you catch them we cook them" philosophy. Tourists and locals alike especially enjoy the Café's homemade pies and salads. After a day lounging by the creek or fishing the White River beneath the majestic bluffs, locals and tourists clamor for the Café's "Coconut Crème Pie" or our "Bacon/Ranch Pasta Salad."

White River Café Bacon/Ranch Pasta Salad
Lead cook Sheila Stetka conjures this pasta salad up for the Café's Salad Bar.
It is a perennial favorite

1 - 16 oz. bag multi-colored spiral pasta, cooked and drained
1 bunch green onions, green part only, diced
Salt and pepper to taste

1 large tomato, diced
1 lb. bacon, cooked and crumbled
1 c. shredded cheddar cheese
1½ c. ranch dressing
1 tsp. red wine vinegar

Directions
Toss all ingredients together, chill minimum of one hour. Serves 8-10 people

Submitted by Sheila Stetka

WHITEWATER GRILL

1310 Hwy. 62 SW St. 2
Mountain Home, AR 72653
(870) 424-3800

The Whitewater Grill offers the finest casual dining in the Twin Lakes Area. A unique atmosphere, friendly service, outstanding steaks, pasta & seafood as well as sandwiches, wraps, salads & soups combine to create a memorable dining experience. All your favorite beverages are available with a simple and free membership application. Open for lunch and dinner for intimate meals or moderate sized parties. Reservations are accepted and you won't be disappointed.

Potato Dijon Soup

¼ c. chopped bacon
⅓ c. diced green peppers
2 Tbsp. minced shallots
¼ c. flour
64 oz. chicken stock
2 pt. heavy cream

⅓ c. diced onion
⅓ c. diced red peppers
¼ c. white wine
¼ c. dijon mustard
2-3 lb. baked, peeled and cubed potatoes
Salt & pepper to taste

Directions

Sautee bacon, onions, peppers and shallots until tender. Add flour and cook stirring for 5 min. Add white wine and reduce to half. Add chicken stock and potatoes, simmer until thickened and potatoes are cooked. Add cream and dijon mustard.

Submitted by Chef Joe and the staff of Whitewater Grill

RESTAURANT

Recipes of

ENTRÉES

BOI DE OURO BRAZILIAN STEAK HOUSE

741 East Van Asche
Fayetteville, AR 72703
(479) 521-1606

"Come to enjoy the complete Brazilian experience as gauchos continuously serve our many choices of prime meats, including steak, pork, lamb, chicken and sausage. We also have a salad bar with your meal that has many unique dishes found only at Boi de Ouro."

Moqueca de Peixe (Brazilian Fish)

6 fresh red snapper filets
3 red tomatoes cut in round slices
1 med. onion cut in round slices
1 red bell pepper, julianne cuts
1 yellow bell pepper, julianne cuts
1 green bell pepper, julianne cuts
200 gr. fresh minced parsley

2 tsp. extra virgin olive oil
2 cans coconut milk
1 tsp. fresh lime juice
1 tsp. black pepper
2 tsp. garlic paste
1 tsp. salt
2 bay leaves

Directions

In a small container mix fresh lime juice, black pepper and salt (to taste). Place filets in marinade for 30 to 35 minutes. Place olive oil and garlic paste into a pan and heat (sauté). Add all peppers and onions and sauté for 3 minutes. Place filets on top of peppers and onions. Then lay tomato slices on top of filets. Add both cans of coconut milk and bay leaves. Cover the pan and cook for 20 minutes over a medium fire. Add minced parsley and heat for 1 to 2 minutes more. This is best served with white rice and a chilled glass of burgundy.

Submitted by Orlando Veronezi, general manager

Bordinos

324 W. Dickson St.
Fayetteville, AR
(479) 527-6795
www.bordinos.com

Bordinos offers a distinctive menu of classic to eclectic cuisine from Chef Chrissy Sanderson. Bordinos' overall look and design, from the vibrant colors, the fanciful doorway with the hand cut metal light sconces, to the original lighting fixtures, is the creation of local artists Kathy Thompson and Eugene Sargent. The Bordinos' menu changes seasonally to include a vast array of unique cuisine. With wine dinners, jazz nights, valet parking and on-line reservations, Bordinos is the premier restaurant in the Northwest Arkansas area.

Scallops and Linguini in a Light White Wine Sauce

1 oz. olive oil
2 tsp. garlic
¼ c. veggie stock or water
6 oz. dry linguini pasta
Salt and pepper to taste
Grated Parmesan cheese if desired

8 oz. scallops
¼ c. white cooking wine
1 small Roma tomato, diced
1 oz. fresh spinach
1 Tbsp. fresh basil, sliced

Directions

Dry off scallops with paper towel to keep from sticking. Heat olive oil in skillet over medium heat until it just starts smoking. Cook scallops on both sides until golden brown. They may need to be loosened with a spatula. Remove scallops and hold until later. Add garlic to pan and cook until nutty brown. Add white wine and veggie stock and reduce liquid by one half. Season with salt, pepper and basil. Add cooked linguini, Roma tomatoes and spinach and toss until not runny but not dry. Distribute onto two plates and top with scallops and grated Parmesan cheese. (2 servings)

Submitted by Joe Fennel, owner

BOTTINI'S RESTAURANT

103 W. Rush
Harrison, AR 72601
(870) 741-4511

Chef Nicholas Bottini is the artisan behind the fine cuisine at Bottini's Restaurant. He is a graduate of the Culinary Institute of America (CIA) in Hyde Park, New York. His Italian/Sicilian parents and grandparents instilled in him a love of fine food which he loves to share with others. His restaurant was featured in Southern Living.

Veal or Chicken Saltimbocca

4-oz.. veal cutlet or 6-oz. chicken breast,
  tenderized (flour to dredge)
Thinly sliced proscuito ham
Thin line of Dijon mustard
2 oz. Mozzarella cheese

1 oz. white wine
2 oz. veal stock
2 Tbsp. whole butter
2 Tbsp. olive oil

Directions

Dredge meat in flour, sauté veal or chicken in olive oil (1 minute for veal, 3 minutes for chicken) (meat should be light brown on one side). Once turned, layer proscuitto, Dijon and Mozzarella on top of meat and put in oven until cheese melts. Remove from sauté pan and put onto plate. Sauce: add wine and veal stock to pan and bring to simmer; add cold butter. Pour sauce over meat, serve.

Submitted by Chef Nicholas Bottini

BRENDA'S SALE BARN CAFE

706 Townsend Dr.
Pocahontas, AR 72455
(870) 892-0240

This has been a Friday favorite for years. People have said they don't like baked fish like this baked fish. We have been baking this fish since 1998. We still have good ole southern fried catfish fillets and catfish steaks served with our homemade hush puppies. Brenda's hours are Mon.-Fri. 6 a.m. - 2 p.m.; Sat. Breakfast Only – 6 a.m. - 11 a.m. Cattle sale is Tuesday at 1:30 p.m. Cafe is open until 8 p.m. on Tuesdays only.

Barn Yard Baked Fish

6-8 catfish fillets (split)
1 Tbsp. Worcestershire sauce
Paprika

¼ c. white cooking wine
Cavenders Greek seasoning

Directions

This makes a ½ buffet. Place fillets in a 9x9 pan. We spray pans with Pam first. Mix wine and Worcestershire sauce together, pour over fillets, making sure you pour a little over each fillet. Sprinkle with Cavenders Greek seasoning until lightly coated. Sprinkle with paprika for color. Bake at 375° for a half hour or so. Yes, no lemon!!

Submitted by Katie and Becky

10 Mountain St
Eureka Springs, AR 72632
(479) 253-6723

Slightly OFF Center at Mountain: Great Food Prepared Fresh Daily! Ice Cold Beer, Wine and Mixed Drinks! Live Music Inside, or on our Enclosed Patio! The Friendliest Locals in Town! Chelsea's Corner Café has been in business for 17 years. We are a local hangout And have built our reputation on catering to Locals, Live Music and Dancing. We are the place where all the misfits - fit and we love to entertain the tourist!

Grilled Red Grouper

8 grouper filets laid out on a cookie sheet
Cover filets with 1 c. olive oil
Mix together:

½ c. paprika	1 Tbsp. cayenne
⅓ c. garlic powder	2 tsp. salt
2 Tbsp. onion powder	2 Tbsp. black powder

Directions

Rub both sides of filets, turning them over in olive oil. When completely covered with rub mix, drop on char grill for 30 seconds. Flip and cook for 30 seconds then flip back (helps fish not to stick). Cook both sides for 2 minutes or until filet is firm. Serve over Basmati rice with orange slice to squeeze over filet and rice.

Submitted by Vicky "Stick" Brown

CHLOE FINE DINING

318 Campbell Ave.
Fayetteville, AR
(479) 442-4144
www.chloefinedining.com

Casual fine dining at Chloe restaurant in Fayetteville, Arkansas features Chef Shawn Keller's classic gourmet Italian fused with world cuisine. Shawn and his wife, Christie, both graduates of the New England Culinary Institute in Vermont, christened their restaurant Chloe (named after their only child) and endeavored to headline a four star act based on the fusion of Fayetteville culture and flavor and their own unique vision. "We try to put the personality of Fayetteville into our restaurant and our food," Chef Keller explains. "People will come back for flavor and everyone here has a sense of responsibility to provide our patrons with a wonderful dining experience."

Chloe Trout

1 trout, cleaned
2 oz. prosciutto, sliced
½ oz. white truffle oil
Flour
2 Tbsp. butter

1 Roma tomato, diced
4 shitake mushrooms, sliced (no stem)
4 Tbsp. olive oil
¼ c. white wine

Directions

Mix diced tomato, prosciutto and shitake together and set aside. Salt and pepper both sides of trout and set aside. Using 2 saute skillets, add 2 tablespoons olive oil to each. Place one skillet on high heat. Coat the trout with flour on both sides. Tap off excess flour to leave a light dusting on the fish. Place trout in the hot oil making sure to lay fish in pan away from you because of splatter. Brown on one side, then turn to brown other side. Add the white wine and take pan off heat. Place other saute pan with 2 tablespoons oil on high heat until warm. Place mushrooms, prosciutto and tomatoes in oil and cook until the prosciutto is slightly crisp. Take pan off heat and place 2 tablespoons butter in the pan and stir until the butter is incorporated into the mixture. Salt and pepper to taste. Pour this mixture over the trout and drizzle the white truffle oil over all. Serve with any side item, like white rice.

Submitted by Shawn Keller, chef

CLIFF HOUSE INN

"Arkansas' Grandest View"
Scenic Highway 7 South
Jasper, AR 72641
(870) 446-2292
www.mcrush.com/cliffhouse

The Cliff House Inn has been written up as an "out of the ordinary, out of the way place." The dining room and our 5 unit motel has a spectacular view of the Arkansas Grand Canyon, the deepest canyon in Arkansas. The Cliff House Inn has been in operation since 1967, serving wonderful home cooking, along with a variety of delicious items on our menu. All of our desserts are homemade. We are famous for our Company's Comin' Pie, and Angel Flake Biscuits. The Cliff House Inn is located 6 miles south of Jasper, AR on scenic Highway 7.

Ritzy Chicken

2 c. Ritz cracker crumbs
¼ c. fresh parsley (chopped)
⅛ tsp. pepper
1 c. melted butter
8 chicken breasts (split)

¾ c. Parmesan cheese
2 tsp. salt
⅛ tsp. minced garlic
⅓ c. sherry

Directions

Blend crumbs, cheese, parsley, salt, pepper, and garlic. Place in shallow dish. Dip each piece of chicken in melted butter and sherry mixture, then roll in crumb mixture. Arrange in shallow pan. Pour remaining butter mixture over chicken. Bake uncovered at 350° for one hour. Do not turn.

Ritzy Chicken in a Sunday favorite at the Cliff House Inn.

Submitted by Becky McLaurin

COOL WATER STEAKS • SEAFOOD • PUB

2217 N. College Ave.
Fayetteville, AR 72701
(479) 571-3636
www.coolwatercafe.com

Cool Water Cafe features an eclectic mix of thick-cut OMAHA steaks, fresh seafood, tasty pastas, signature sandwiches, crisp salads and tempting desserts served by the friendliest people. Open for lunch and dinner 7 days a week plus our famous Sunday Brunch. For business lunches, a special dinner or a family outing, you can't beat the atmosphere or the value. And our private banquet room comfortably seats 100, perfect for receptions, parties or conferences.

Rosemary Tomato Chicken Pasta

1 Tbsp. butter
½ c. sliced mushrooms
1 oz. sundried tomatoes, diced fine
1 Tbsp. chopped green onion
⅛ c. red wine
⅛ c. Parmesan cheese, grated
Salt and pepper to taste

3 oz. chicken pieces, pounded flat
1 Tbsp. minced garlic
1 Tbsp. fresh rosemary
½ c. diced red bell pepper
½ c. heavy cream
6 oz. linguini, prepared according to
package directions

Directions

Pound and flour chicken pieces. In a large skillet, melt butter. Add chicken pieces and diced red pepper. Flip chicken and add mushrooms and garlic. When chicken is almost done, add rosemary, green onion, sundried tomatoes, red wine, cream and Parmesan. Allow to reduce. When sauce is thick, combine with cooked pasta.

Submitted by Jared Hickman, sous chef

COOL WATER STEAKS • SEAFOOD • PUB

STEAKS•SEAFOOD•PUB

2217 N. College Ave.
Fayetteville, AR 72701
(479) 571-3636
www.coolwatercafe.com

Cool Water Cafe features an eclectic mix of thick-cut OMAHA steaks, fresh seafood, tasty pastas, signature sandwiches, crisp salads and tempting desserts served by the friendliest people. Open for lunch and dinner 7 days a week plus our famous Sunday Brunch. For business lunches, a special dinner or a family outing, you can't beat the atmosphere or the value. And our private banquet room comfortably seats 100, perfect for receptions, parties or conferences.

Seafood Pasta

1 - 4 oz. salmon filet
½ c. chopped crab meat
½ c. red onion, diced
1 Tbsp. minced garlic
½ lemon
½ c. heavy cream
6 oz. fettuccini pasta, cooked according
   to package directions

10-12 small shrimp
½ c. green bell pepper, diced
⅛ c. red bell pepper
⅛ c. white wine
1½ Tbsp. basil pesto
⅛ c. Parmesan cheese, grated
1 Tbsp. butter
Salt and pepper to taste

Directions

Melt butter in a large pan. Add salmon, green and red peppers and onions. Flip salmon. Add garlic and shrimp. When shrimp are almost done, add crab meat, lemon, pesto, white wine, cream and Parmesan. Allow to reduce. Toss with hot pasta and serve.

Submitted by Jared Hickman, sous chef

301 Southridge Blvd.
Heber Springs, AR 72543
(501) 362-5712

Cowboy Club House will tickle anyones taste buds. We offer Daily Lunch Specials, Home Cookin', BBQ, and really healthy menu items for those that want to tighten the ol' belt buckle. We also offer Blue Bell ice cream, old fashioned shakes, and homemade pies for dessert. Not only do we offer a, Kiss Your Grandma, good lunch but we serve breakfast on the weekends and breakfast all day on Sunday. So ya'll saddle up your horsepower and come on in, we look forward to seeing ya.

Cowboy Chicken

6 - 4-6 oz. boneless skinless chicken breasts
16 oz. sour cream
2 bags of boil-in-bag white rice

8 oz. pkg. cream cheese
2 - 8 oz. cans cream of chicken soup
1 jar dried beef

Directions

Preheat oven to 350˚.

In a bowl mix: cream cheese, cream of chicken and sour cream until smooth. In a 9x13 glass baking dish place dried beef along the bottom of dish then arrange the chicken on top of the beef. Pour creamy mixture on top of chicken, cover with aluminum foil and place in oven for 1 hour then uncover and bake for an additional 15 min. Follow the box directions for boiling the rice. Serves 6

Submitted by Ashley Blankenship, owner

ELLA'S RESTAURANT AT THE INN AT CARNALL

1905 ELLA'S RESTAURANT 2003

465 N. Arkansas Ave.
Fayetteville, AR 72701
(479) 521-0401

Located at the historic Inn at Carnall Hall on the corner of the University of Arkansas' beautiful campus, Ella's Restaurant offers exquisite fine dining with a pinch of history. The cuisine features classic French procedures with modern French style. We use only local produce brought in daily and the highest quality meats and fish available. Open for breakfast, lunch, and dinner Monday-Saturday, as well as for Sunday brunch. Come experience something better.

This recipe is a representation of what we call "country French" cooking. The combination of orange, garlic, cabbage, and sausage go extremely well with pheasant. At the restaurant this dish is served with a butternut squash puree and baby green beans sautéed with chopped bacon, but mash potatoes and regular green beans would work just as well. This is a fun dish to do with a wonderful aroma that will encapsulate your entire house from the minute you put the pheasant in the oven.

Orange Marinated Pheasant wrapped in Boudin Blanc and Cabbage with Chestnut Beurre Noir

For Marinade:

1 c. orange juice
1 Tbsp. garlic, chopped
1 tsp. paprika
2 - 8 oz. pheasant breasts, skin on

Zest of one orange
1 Tbsp. white wine vinegar
½ c. extra virgin olive oil

Combine all ingredients in mixing bowl and whisk together. Transfer to zip lock bag. Add pheasant and allow to marinate for at least one hour. .

To Finish:

1 Tbsp. butter & 1 Tbsp. olive oil for frying   1 head napa cabbage
1 pkg. white sausage, thinly sliced (bratwurst will work)
Salt and pepper to taste

Directions

Preheat oven to 325.

In a medium non-stick sauté pan heat butter and olive oil over medium-high heat. Season pheasant breast on both sides with salt and pepper. Sauté pheasant, skin side down, until browned. Transfer to a baking dish, skin side up, and roast pheasant in oven for twenty minutes. Remove from oven and set aside.

Recipe continued on next page

Orange Marinated Pheasant ...continued

Meanwhile, boil water in a medium sauté pan. Trim cabbage, cutting leaves free from hard stalk. You will only need four leaves, so reserve rest of cabbage for another use (it's great in salad or sautéed in butter and white wine!). Add leaves to boiling water and cook until soft, about three minutes. Transfer to ice bath until cool, then drain on paper towels.

Lay pheasant on working surface skin side up. Layer white sausage on top of breasts, covering the entire top side. Take blanched cabbage and wrap it around pheasant and sausage, using one leaf for the top and one for the bottom, and fixing both together with a toothpick.

Transfer back to baking dish and place back in oven for five minutes, until cabbage is golden brown on top. Serve immediately drizzled with buerre noir.

Chestnut Buerre Noir

   1 c. butter

In a medium sauce pan melt butter over medium heat. Continue to heat butter on medium heat for around ten minutes, whisking occasionally. Butter should turn a "chestnut" color and have a slightly nutty aroma when finished. Keep in a warm place until ready to use. Whisk vigorously before use.

Makes two main course servings

Submitted by Travis D. Maier, executive culinary artist,
and Aaron Nix, assistant culinary artist

EUREKA PIZZA

(479) 444-8282 ext. 105
Fayetteville, AR 72702
www.eurekapizza.com

Eureka Pizza started in 1992 in Fayetteville. We're proud to have been voted "Best Pizza" 5 years in a row by the 54,000 readers of the Northwest Arkansas Times newspaper. Starting in June 2006 Eureka Pizza added more cheese and more toppings to every pizza. We have been called "Gourmet Pizzas at Eureka Prices". We now offer healthy new toppings like Roma tomatoes, spinach and grilled chicken. We also offer single pizza pricing for your convenience. We're still proud to offer the "best Deal in town! Give us a call soon!!

Spinach & Tomato Pizza with Pesto Sauce

Eureka Pizza Dough:
1 pkg. active dry yeast
1 c. warm water (105° F)
3½ c. bread flour (12% protein)

2 tsp. sugar
¼ c. vegetable oil
2 tsp. sea salt

Directions

In a mixing bowl, combine yeast, sugar, water and vegetable oil. Add the flour and salt and mix, using a dough hook, until the dough comes away from the sides and moves up the dough hook (do not over mix- will make crust tough). Remove the dough. Oil the bowl with vegetable oil and put the dough back in the bowl. Cover the bowl and let the dough rise until doubled in size, about 1 hour or so. Turn the dough out onto a floured surface and divide dough in half. Roll the dough into balls, cover, and let the dough rest for 15 to 20 minutes. Yield 2 12" pizzas

Form into skin with raised edges (handle or crust edge) we use screens for our dough or a lightly oiled cookie sheet or pizza pan will work (no oil is needed if you use a screen for baking.) Preheat Oven to 400 degrees F.

Pesto (buy a quality brand like Villa Belmonte) or make your own:
¼ c. chopped fresh basil leaves
1 large garlic clove, finely chopped
2 Tbsp.Parmesan cheese
Fresh ground black pepper to taste

2 Tbsp. toasted pine nuts
Sea salt to taste
2 Tbsp. olive oil (virgin or extra virgin)

Recipe continued on next page

Spinach & Tomato Pizza with Pesto Sauce...continued

Spinach

1 c. (fresh- compacted in cup- or frozen) If frozen- thaw- squeeze out as much water as possible	½ c. ricotta cheese
	½ tsp. fresh ground pepper
1/2 teaspoon granulated garlic	½ tsp. Sea salt

Combine ingredients- mix well- do not over mix.

4 Roma Tomatoes- sliced approx. ⅓" thick.

Cheese 7 oz. quality, shredded 100 % real mozzarella cheese.

Pizza Assembly

Spread pesto on crust- ¼- ⅓ c. – spread evenly

Place spinach on top of pesto- spinach/ricotta mix will be sticky- place evenly for best results. Place cheese on spinach- spread evenly- avoid crust handle

Place sliced Roma tomatoes evenly on top of cheese- bake at 400 degrees F until done (about 15 minutes or until cheese is brown and bubbly)

Remove and enjoy! Bon Appetit!!!

Classic White Pizza

Eureka Pizza Dough Recipe	Pesto
Mozzarella Cheese	

Form pizza crust, spread pesto, apply shredded cheese evenly- bake at 400 degrees F until crust is brown and cheese is bubbly- enjoy with tossed salad and a nice glass of Chardonnay! Enjoy!

Submitted by Rolf Wilkin, owner

Fireside Grill & Catering

1508 Highway 62 East
Mountain Home, AR 72653
(870) 425-5525

Fireside Grill & Catering opened its doors for business on June 6, 2006. The restaurant's hours of operation are: Tuesday – Saturday 5:30 a.m. to 9:00 p.m. and Sunday 7:00 a.m. to 2:00 p.m. Fireside Grill offers breakfast, lunch, dinner, and catering services. The newly remodeled building features two hand painted murals by a local artist. Fireside Grill offers a variety of breakfast, lunch, and dinner specials daily.

Sausage & Peppers Meatloaf

1½ c. Barilla sweet peppers & garlic pasta sauce
1 lb. ground beef
¾ c. Parmesan cheese, grated
2 tsp. garlic, minced
½ tsp. Pepper

1 lb. hot or sweet Italian pork sausage, removed from casings
¾ c. breadcrumbs
1 egg
½ tsp. Salt

Directions

Mix ½ cup pasta sauce with remaining ingredients in a large bowl until well blended. Form into serving-sized loaves. Place in baking dish. With a spoon, place an indention on top of each loaf. Spoon remaining 1 cup of sauce on top of loaves. Bake at 400° for 30-35 minutes or until done.

Note: You may want to heat remaining sauce from jar and serve with cooked meatloaves.

Submitted by Brent Smith, owner

FRED'S HICKORY INN

"Keeping the Tradition Alive"
1502 N. Walton Blvd.
Bentonville, AR 72712
(479) 273-3303

Fred's Hickory Inn was started with the idea that "if we can serve quality food, offer good service and provide a comfortable atmosphere people will dine with us." Thirty-six years later we still slow smoke our meats on Fred's Original Smoker. We use the best quality meat available. Our steaks and chops are hand cut and grilled to perfection. And, of course, our spaghetti and cheesecake are Miss Lou's original recipe.

Sherry and the staff at Fred's are committed to keep the tradition that our founders and friends, Fred and Lou Gaye, started in 1970 alive for future generations.

Sherry's Artichoke Chicken

6 boneless chicken breasts	5 Tbsp. butter
1 Tbsp. chopped garlic	1 whole onion, chopped
1 to 2 cans artichoke hearts	⅓ c. flour
1½ tsp. rosemary	1½ tsp. salt
¼ tsp. pepper	1 c. chicken broth
1 c. dry white wine or another c. of broth	1 c. sliced mushrooms

Directions

Melt butter and garlic in skillet. Sauté chicken until lightly browned. Transfer chicken to a 9x13 baking dish and add onions to skillet. blend in flour, rosemary, salt and pepper. Add broth and wine stirring until thick. Add mushrooms. Spoon over chicken. Bake at 375° for 20 to 30 minutes. Serve with a wild rice blend.

Submitted by Sherry Mendenhall, owner

HARDY OLDE TOWN CAFE

107 East Main St
Hardy, AR 72542
(870) 856-3177

Olde Hardy Café specializes in Homemade Fried Pies, Fried Green Tomatoes, Sweet Potato Fries, and the best Catfish in Olde Hardy Town as well as our daily lunch specials. We are open Thurs, Fri, Sat & Mon 7:30 a.m.-3p.m. & Sun 7:30-2p.m. Closed Tues & Wed.

Dee Dee's Favorite Meatloaf

3 lb. hamburger
1 c. ketchup
¼ c. green pepper (chopped)
Salt & pepper to taste

2 eggs
½ c. onions (chopped)
8 slices toast (torn in small pieces)

Directions

Preheat oven to 350°. Add all ingredients together. Mix very well. Form into loaf and place in baking dish.

Pour ketchup over the top. Bake for 25-30 minutes. Let cool a bit before slicing.

Submitted by LaReva Wiles, owner

HOG HAUS BREWING CO.

430 W. Dickson St.
Fayetteville, AR
(479) 521-BREW
www.hoghaus.com

From special Haus-made Ales, to an array of traditional and eclectic appetizers, to soups, salads, sandwiches, pizzas, steak, fish and more, Hog Haus has something for everyone. Hog Haus Brewing Company has a complete bar with domestic and imported beer on tap as well, making it a great place to enjoy a cold one–inside the beautiful building, or on their famous balcony. Stop in on Saturday afternoons and enjoy a brewery tour & beer tasting. "This facility is a landmark and is the only operating brewery in the Northwest Arkansas area. It has a fantastic location and the architecture is beautiful inside and out. The brewery itself is top notch and it sports two full kitchens. With all of this combined, we feel it will brings something great to the area," says co-owner Kari Larson.

Shrimp & Grits

1 lb. peeled shrimp
⅛ c. Worcestershire
3 tomatoes, diced
8 oz. white wine
2 Tbsp. minced garlic

¼ c. green onions, sliced
½ stick butter
2 Tbsp. Tabasco
½ c. cooked bacon
Salt and pepper to taste

Grits
1 c. grits
1 c. water
Salt and pepper to taste

2 c. milk
4 oz. cheese

Directions

In a large saute pan, cook shrimp, garlic and remaining ingredients in pan until shrimp turns pink. For grits: Bring liquid to a boil and whisk in dry ingredients until thick. Place small portion of grits into serving bowl and spoon over grits. (Serves 4)

Submitted by Kari Larson and Julie Sill, co-owners

Hot Dog Alley
& other good things

NW Arkansas' Home of the Gourmet Dogs!

2201 E Central #1
Bentonville, AR 72712
(479) 271-6633

Choose from over a dozen different ways to top your dog! Offering a family and wholesome environment with fast friendly service. Other good things include panini style sandwiches, Bratwursts, Polish Links, Italian Beef Sandwiches, and much more. Closed Sundays. You can find us in Bentonville: From the 540 By-Pass, exit 88 (Pea Ridge, Bentonville) and head West towards town (approx 1.2 miles). Go thru the light at Moberly and we are located in the Central Park Plaza on the right. Or in Lowell: From the 540 By-Pass, exit 78 (Rogers, Lowell) and head East about 1 mile. We are located inside the Phillips 66 station at the corner of Hwy 71B and 264.

The Arkansas Dog

8 hot dog buns   8 hot dog franks

Directions

Top each w/mustard, chili, sauerkraut and shredded cheese.

Toast under the broiler for about 1 minute (optional).

Serves 4 to 8 (depending on how many each person will eat!)

Submitted by Mama Wienie

9999 Edgemont Road
Edgemont, AR 72044
(501) 723-4480

Janssen's Lakefront Restaurant has been in business since 1979. We are on beautiful Greers Ferry Lake in North Central Arkansas. We specialize in steaks and fresh fish, and the menu has something for everyone. Come see us by car or drive your boat up to the boat dock.

Shrimp Creole with White Rice

½ lemon, sliced
2 lb. shrimp, unpeeled
2 Tbsp. butter
1 c. onion, chopped
¼ c. parsley, chopped
⅔ can tomatoes, canned #10
2⅝ tsp. lemon juice
1 tsp. salt
¼ tsp. crushed red pepper
½ tsp. thyme
White rice, cooked

4 whole black peppercorns
4 slices bacon
1 clove garlic
1½ c. green pepper, chopped
1½ c. celery, sliced
6 oz. tomato paste
2⅝ tsp. sugar
¼ tsp. black pepper
1 bay leaf
½ tsp. file powder

Directions

Into 1 qt. boiling water, add lemon slices, black peppercorns and shrimp. Reduce heat, simmer, uncovered for 3 minutes. Drain shrimp, reserve 1 cup cooking liquid. Sauté bacon over low heat, until crisp. Remove and crumble. To bacon fat add butter, garlic, onion, green pepper, parsley, celery; cook, stirring, until tender. Add shrimp liquid, bacon, tomatoes, tomato paste, lemon juice, sugar, salt, pepper, red pepper, bay leaf, and thyme; Bring to boil. Reduce heat; simmer, covered, 30 minutes. Just before serving, stir in file powder and shrimp, bring to boiling. Reduce heat and simmer 5 minutes. Serve over hot, cooked white rice.

Submitted by Tim Janssen

**6 miles north of Mtn. View on Hwy. 5
at Jack's White River Fishing Resort
Mountain View, AR 72560
(870) 585-2121**

Jo Jo's Catfish Wharf was established in 1995. Located on the bank of the White River amid Jack's Fishing Resort, the restaurant offers scenic river view dining. The specialty of this family-oriented establishment is catfish fillets, however, one will find many other menu items that would delight anyone's taste buds.

Fried Trout

6 fresh rainbow trout
  (heads and skin on)*
Fresh lemon juice
Garlic powder

Salt and pepper
¾ stick butter, not margarine
Cornmeal
Flour

Directions

Mix some cornmeal and flour in a 3:1 ratio in a shallow dish. Squeeze lemon juice over trout and inside cavity. Sprinkle inside cavity with garlic powder, salt and pepper. Roll in meal and flour mixture to which salt and pepper (a dash of each) has been added. Melt butter in heavy skillet. Place trout in pan and place lid n top until first side is browned. Turn trout over and remove lid; brown the second side. Trout is cooked perfectly when meat pulls away from the bones, leaving the skeleton of the fish intact.

*The flavor of the fish is better if cooked with heads on (you may remove eyes before cooking!) Heads may be removed before serving if desired.

Note: This is Aunt Mary's popular recipe at their fishing resort in Mountain View, Arkansas.

Submitted by Jo & Mike Mitchell, owners

OZARK RESTAURANT

Hwy. 5 & 9 North
Next to White River Hoedown
Mountain View, AR 72560
(870) 269-4136

Joshua's Ozark Restaurant was established in 1985 and has been a part of this small town ever since. We promote a family atmosphere with a friendly staff and home cooking just like mama used to do it. We have live music on the weekends, free of charge to anyone dining with us and large dining rooms for any of your family's needs or any other groups that need lots of seating. Groups of more than 20 please call for reservations.

Chicken and Dumplings

1 gal. chicken broth in large pan
2 eggs
1 tsp. cavanders
6 c. cooked, deboned & skinless chicken,
   cut into bite size pieces

2 c. self-rising flour
2 c. broth
⅛ tsp. nutmeg

Directions

In a large bowl, mix flour and spices. Add eggs one at a time. Mix well. Add broth, a little at a time until moist enough to handle. On flour-covered table, knead dough until it no longer sticks to your hands. Bring to a rolling boil. Roll out dough to ¼" thickness, cut into bite size pieces. Drop into boiling broth, stirring well to keep from clumping. Cook dumplings for about 20 minutes on low simmer. Add chicken. Turn off and let set with an occasional stir for about 10 minutes. Serve hot.

Submitted by Fred Hubbard, owner

MAMA Z's CAFE

357 W. Henri De Tonti Blvd.
Tontitown, AR 72770
(479) 361-2750
www.mamazs.net

Mama Z's opened in May 1988 accomplishing a life-long dream of Edna (Morsani) Zulpo to have a cafe using many old recipes handed down from Edna's Nonna (grandmother). Mama Z's serves breakfast, lunch and dinner offering homemade pastas, sauces, rolls and jellies.

Mama Z's Italian Meatballs

2 lbs. lean ground beef
1 tsp. salt
½ tsp. black pepper
4 cloves garlic or 1 Tbsp. minced garlic
¼ c. dry bread crumbs or oats

2 eggs, beaten
4 Tbsp. finely chopped onion
2 Tbsp. finely chopped celery
2 Tbsp. dry Italian seasoning

Directions

Mix all ingredients except ground beef. Add mixture to ground beef and mix. Do not overmix as it will make your meatballs tough. Roll ¼ cup of meat mixture into a ball. Makes about 16 meatballs.

Place meatballs in a baking dish and bake 35 to 45 minutes on 350°. Add meatballs to spaghetti sauce in saucepan and simmer on low heat for approximately 30 minutes before serving.

Submitted by Edna Zulpo

Master Chef

1225 Main St.
Harrison, AR 72601
(870) 741-6023

Master Chef was established in 1968 and is home owned and operated. Master Chef features home style cooking. Selections include Mexican food, fried chicken, sandwiches, catfish, cashew chicken, salads, kids menus and a whole lot more. Master Chef is open 7 days a week from 10 a.m. to 8 p.m.

Jerry's Ranch Burgers

3 lb. lean ground beef
1 c. chopped onions
21 oz. ketchup
A little hot water

2 tsp. salt
1 tsp. chili powder
Pepper to taste

Directions

Brown beef and onion (drain fat). Add rest of ingredients and just enough hot water to give it a Sloppy Joe consistency. Cook 15-20 minutes.

Submitted by Burlene Hinson, owner

OZARK MOUNTAIN SMOKE HOUSE

Farmington, AR 72730
(800) 643-3437

In 1946 a small smokehouse was built by Roy Sharp and the Ozark Mountain Smoke House was launched as a business/hobby(?). In 1962 Roy's son, Frank, and his wife, Sara, became actively involved in the business, which they still operate (with their four children) on the Sharp farm on the slopes of Mount Kessler. Visitors are cordially invited to visit Mount Kessler and the smokehouse and kitchens of the Ozark Mountain Family.

Smoked Turkey Divan

6 stalks cooked broccoli (trimmed)
1½ Tbsp. melted butter or margarine
2 Tbsp. grated Parmesan cheese
2 Tbsp. dry sherry
6 slices smoked turkey, cut ½" thick
1½ c. white sauce

3 eggs yolks
1½ Tbsp. sour cream
½ tsp. salt
⅛ tsp. pepper
2 Tbsp. grated Parmesan cheese
1½ Tbsp. dry sherry

Directions

Rub a 7x11" baking dish with butter. Arrange trimmed cooked broccoli crosswise on bottom. Sprinkle over melted butter, the 2 Tbsp. grated Parmesan cheese and the 2 Tbsp. dry sherry. Cover broccoli with sliced turkey. Beat together white sauce, egg yolks, sour cream, salt and pepper. Spoon this over sliced turkey. Dust over the additional Parmesan, and sprinkle with the additional sherry. Bake about 15 minutes at 350°.

Ham with Sweet Potatoes and Pineapple

2 lbs. center cut ham slice 1" thick
2 or 3 halved sweet potatoes
1½ c. undrained pineapple chunks
¼ c. undiluted orange juice

¼ c. water
¼ c. brown sugar
2 Tbsp. cornstarch
¼ tsp. cinammon, if desired

Directions

Preheat oven to 350° F. Put ham slice in bottom of 1½ qt. casserole. Arrange sweet potatoes around ham. In small pan combine pineapple, orange juice, water, brown sugar, cornstarch and cinnamon. Mix well. Cook over low heat, stirring constantly, until mixture thickens and comes to a boil. Spoon sauce over ham and sweet potatoes. Bake uncovered at 350° for 40 to 50 minutes until sweet potatoes become tender.

Submitted by Ozark Mountain Family Cookbook

Pied Piper Pub & Inn

82 Armstrong
Eureka Springs, AR
(479) 363-9976

Dublin Coddle is often referred to as the "drunk man's best friend" because of its hardiness and the way it sticks to your ribs and fills you up. It is traditionally served with homemade soda bread. The Pub is open 7 days a week serving food from noon to midnight.

Dublin Coddle

1 lb. bacon bits and pieces
3 large potatoes, peeled and sliced thin
½ Tbsp. salt
¼ Tbsp. sage
⅛ tsp. ground clove
½ tsp. all spice

1 lb. Italian sausage, cubed
5 onions sliced thin
¼ Tbsp. pepper
⅛ tsp. ground ginger
⅛ tsp. mace
½ c. water

Directions

Mix all dried spices together. You will stack the layers of the following ingredients seasoning each layer as you go. The first layer is ½ of the onions on an ungreased casserole or baking dish. Season and lay down ⅓ of the potatoes. Season and layer with ½ of the sausage and bacon. Season and layer with the rest of the onions, season and layer with ⅓ of the potato, season, meat, season, potatoes and finish off the season. Add the water, pouring it down the side of the pan so you don't wash off the seasoning. Cover with parchment paper, tucking it into the sides and top with tin foil. bake at 350° about 1 hour or until potatoes are tender.

Submitted by Fatima Swallow, owner

POWERHOUSE SEAFOOD & GRILL

112 N. University
Fayetteville, AR 72701
(479) 442-8300

A former electric power company from the early 1900s, Powerhouse Seafood offers a unique and entertaining casual atmosphere that has been award-winning since the doors were reopened in 1992. With private banquet rooms, outside live entertainment and a large variety of menu options with daily dinner and drink specials, Powerhouse Seafood can take care of all of your dining needs.

Ponchartain Fish

8 oz. fish
¼ c. crabmeat
For sauce:
4 lbs. butter
3 c. madeira wine
1 lb. margarine
¼ c. Kitchen Bouquet

⅛ c. shrimp

1 cookspoon chicken base
1½ gal. water
4 c. flour

Directions

Melt the butter, add the chicken base, along with the wine and the Kitchen Bouquet. Bring to a boil, add the water and bring to a boil. Melt the 1 lb. of margarine and add the 4 c. of flour to make a roux. Mix in with the wine sauce until it thickens. Serves 100 people.

Pan broil your fish cooked to your desire. In a sauté pan add ⅛ c. of cooked shrimp, ¼ c. crabmeat. Add one ladle of the sauce and sauté together. Pour over the pan broil fish and enjoy.

Submitted by Cortney Richardson, prep cook

RED APPLE INN AND COUNTRY CLUB

RED APPLE INN
AND COUNTRY CLUB

1000 Country Club Road
Heber Springs, AR 72543
1-800-RED-APPLE
www.redappleinn.com

The Red Apple Inn Resort is located in the foothills of the Ozark Mountains on beautiful Greer's Ferry Lake. We offer fine dining with an assortment of steaks, seafood, and homemade dessert in our dining room overlooking the lake. The Inn was designed by a student of Frank Lloyd Wright and blends in with the natural surroundings of Eden Isle.

Southwest Spiced Lamb Chop with Raspberry Glaze

1 qt. olive oil
¼ c. pepper, ground
1⅓ Tbsp. cayenne

½ c. chili powder
½ c. cumin seed, toasted and ground
½ c. paprika

Glaze:

1 qt. raspberries, pureed
1½ tsp. chili powder
½ c. honey
2 Tbsp. lemon juice
½ tsp. salt

2 jalapenos, sliced
1 tsp. cayenne
½ c. sugar
1 pint, water

Directions

Combine all ingredients except lamb. Rub mix over chops and leave to marinade. Grill to taste. When chop is cooked, brush with glaze. Place back on grill to caramelize. Then brush again before putting on serving plate.

Glaze: combine all ingredients and simmer until thick. Needs to be low heat. Reduce and strain through mesh. The seasoning mixture may be cut in half.

Submitted by David Smith

RIVER GRILLE STEAKHOUSE

STEAKHOUSE

1003 McClain Road
Bentonville, AR 72712
(479) 271-4141

Touted as one of the state's finest restaurants by local newspaper readers, the River Grille is an experience for the senses! The menu features center of the plate hand-cut U.S.D.A. prime aged beef and fresh fish flown in daily. Creative and exciting daily special prepared by talented chefs and an extensive wine list of over 200 bottles of fines wines, which has received the Award of Excellence from Wine Spectator for five consecutive years.

Fresh Grilled Swordfish Piccata on Cilantro Basmati Rice with sautéed asparagus tips, artichoke hearts, and Roma tomatoes

Four 8-oz. swordfish steaks, ½" thick

Cilantro Basmarti Rice

½ c. diced white onion
2½ c. water
½ Tbsp. salt
2 Tbsp. butter

½ c. chopped fresh cilantro
1 c. Basmati rice
1 tsp. black pepper
½ Tbsp. chopped garlic

In a wide, heavy bottomed stock pot, melt the butter until it begins to brown. Add garlic and onions, stir and sauté 5 minutes. Add the remaining ingredients, bring to a boil, stir, cover tightly, reduce heat, simmer for 20 minutes.

Vegetables

2 Tbsp. olive oil
1 bunch fresh asparagus (cut in 1" pieces)
3 Roma tomatoes, quartered

1 Tbsp. chopped garlic
1 c. canned artichoke hearts
Salt and pepper

Heat the olive oil, add the garlic, sauté until it begins to brown. Add the asparagus and artichoke hearts, sauté 5 minutes. Add the Roma tomatoes, sauté 5 minutes more. Season to taste with salt and pepper.

Recipe continued on next page

Fresh Grilled Swordfish Piccata...continued

Piccata Sauce:

1 c. dry white wine, pref. white Bordeaux	Juice of ½ lemon
3 Tbsp. capers	½ c. butter
2 Tbsp. minced shallots	Salt and pepper to taste

In a sauce pan, begin by reducing the white wine with shallots, lemon juice and capers. Continue to simmer and reduce until only ½ cup liquid remains. Reduce the heat, and add the butter while slowly swirling the pan to incorporate. Season to taste with salt and pepper.

Preheat the grill, season the swordfish steaks with salt and pepper. Place them on the grill for 5 minutes, turn over and cook 5 minutes more. Check for doneness. If necessary, cook 2 or 3 minutes more on each side, being careful not to overcook. Remove to a warm plate.

Presentation:

Place ½ cup basmati rice in the center of 4 plates. Lean the sword fish steak against the rice, and spoon the sauce over the fish and around the rice. Place the asparagus, artichoke hearts, and Roma tomatoes around the rice. Garnish with fresh lemon wedges and fresh cilantro leaves.

Submitted by Brenda Swango, owner

ROGUE'S MANOR AT SWEET SPRING

124 Spring St.
Eureka Springs, AR 72632
(479) 253-4911
www.roguesmanor.com

Housed in an 1874 Victorian house built into a cliff in the steep hills of historic Eureka Springs, Rogue's Manor offers a fine dining experience with a chic antique motif. We pride ourselves on the variety and freshness of our offerings and are famous for our steak and lobster. An extensive wine list complements the menu. The Hideaway Lounge offers premium liquors and large single-malt Scotch selection in a plush atmosphere of leather, velvet and redwood. In addition, 4 suites are available for an intimate overnight get-a-way. The Lounge opens at 3 p.m. Dinner seating is from 5 p.m to 9 p.m.

Greek Chicken

1 oz. olive oil
Flour for dusting chicken
2 oz. chopped tomatoes
1 oz. kalamta olives
1 tsp. basil
1 tsp. garlic, granulated
2 tsp. pernod or ouzo
2 oz. chicken stock

7 oz. chicken breast
2 oz. sliced mushrooms
2 oz. diced green onions
½ oz. capers
1 tsp. oregano
2 tsp. white wine
1 oz. feta cheese, crumbled
Salt and white pepper

Directions

Heat the oil in an 8" skillet. Dredge the chicken in flour and place in the heated skillet. Cook on medium heat. Brown chicken on one side, turn over to brown. Add white wine and pernod. The pernod may flame. Add mushrooms, tomatoes, green onions, olives, capers, plus all of the seasonings. Then pour chicken stock over all. Lift the chicken so the vegetables are under the chicken. Continue to cook until chicken is cooked. Place the chicken on a plate. Pour the resulting sauce over the chicken. Top with feta cheese. Bon Appetit!

Submitted by Chef Debbie Sederstrom, co-owner

SMOKEY BONES BARBEQUE & GRILL

643 E. Van Asche Dr
Fayetteville AR 72703
(479) 251-7517

Resembling a rustic mountain lodge, Smokey Bones Barbeque & Grill serves award-winning barbeque and a broad variety of other American favorites. Its menu features slow-smoked Baby-Back and St. Louis-style ribs, hand-pulled pork, sliced beef brisket, choice steaks, grilled chicken and fish, fresh salads, sandwiches, Buffalo burgers and Angus burgers. Some appetizers and side offerings include Barbeque Chicken Nachos, Old-Fashioned Skillet Corn Bread with crushed pecan butter, green beans and cinnamon apples. Guests also enjoy the restaurant's signature dessert – a bag of fresh "made-to-order" hot cinnamon-sugar doughnuts served with strawberry dipping sauce.

Grilled Mahi-Mahi Sandwich with Cajun Remoulade

Mahi-mahi seasoning (recipe below)
4 pieces fresh mahi-mahi, skinless (approx. 6-8 oz. each)
4 Kaiser rolls, toasted
1 tomato, sliced
1 lemon, cut into 4 wedges

Cajun remoulade (recipe below)
4 pieces green leaf lettuce
2 Tbsp. melted butter

Seasoning:
1½ tsp. garlic powder
1½ tsp. dried oregano
½ tsp. salt

1½ tsp. dried basil
1 tsp. dried rosemary
⅛ tsp. pepper

Combine and mix all ingredients in a small bowl and set aside.

Cajun Remoulade:
½ c. mayonnaise
1 Tbsp. Dijon mustard

2 Tbsp. pickle relish
1 Tbsp. blackening seasoning

Combine ingredients in a mixing bowl, mix thoroughly and then place in refrigerator to chill.

Completion: Preheat gas or charcoal grill to medium-high heat. Season mahi-mahi with approximately ½ Tbsp. seasoning and place on pre-heated grill. Cook approximately 4-5 minutes on each side, rotating once per side to create diamond marks. Cook until internal temperature reaches 145° F. Brush each piece of fish with melted butter just before removing from grill. Remove mahi-mahi from grill and place on toasted Kaiser roll bottom. Top each with one piece of lettuce, one tomato slice and bun top. Serve with Cajun remoulade and lemon wedge on the side.

Submitted by Smokey Bones team

SPAVINAW SUPPER CLUB

11662 N. Highway 59
Gravette, AR 72736
(479) 787-7300

This restaurant is located in a traditional century-old Ozark farmhouse that has been restored. It is surrounded by a 700-acre ranch divided by Spavinaw Creek, which is fed upstream by natural springs. There is no entertainment at the club, just gracious dining in the three dining rooms or, when weather permits, on a deck overlooking the stream. Dinner only is served Tuesday through Saturday from 5 p.m. to 10 p.m.

Reservations suggested. Closed Mondays and the month of January. The club is owned and operated by John and Janice Lykins. It is located 2 miles south of Gravette on State Highway 59 South.

Chateaubriand

1½ lb. cut of beef tenderloin, trimmed
8 large broccoli flowerets
4 large mushroom buttons
2 Tbsp. butter
6 egg yolks
Salt and nutmeg to taste

40 baby Belgian carrots
4 medium tomatoes, halved and stuffed
   with Mozzarella cheese
1 oz. rum flambé
6 large potatoes

Directions

Boil and mash potatoes, whip in eggs yolks and a "suspicion" of nutmeg. Season to taste with salt. Using a 14-inch pastry bag, pipe a border around a heat-proof or metal platter. Sprinkle potatoes with paprika and bake 10 minutes at 350°. Broil tenderloin to desired doneness (12 to 15 minutes for medium rare). Lightly broil tomatoes. Steam broccoli and carrots until tender crisp. Sauté mushrooms about 2 minutes in a little butter. Place tenderloin in center of plaster and surround with vegetables. Pour rum flambé over meat. Light, let flame burn out, then carve at tables. Serves 4.

Submitted by Nancy Kennedy

373 Dave Creek Parkway
Fairfield Bay, AR 72088
(501) 884-4700

Stevenson's Restaurant is a casual restaurant that features home-cooked meals and home-made desserts. This is the first recipe I ever made and everyone seems to like it.

Chicken Marsala

4-boneless chicken breasts
1 pkg. demi glaze
1 Portabella mushroom, chopped
Egg wash
¼ c. heavy whipping cream

Slice Provolone cheese
4 Tbsp. Marcella wine
3 c. of flour
6 Tbsp. butter
Salt and pepper to taste

Directions

Coat chicken in flour and egg wash twice. Mix 1 pkg. of demi glaze with 4 Tbsp. Marsala wine. Bring to a boil. Add 1 chopped Portabella mushroom and ¼ c. heavy whipping cream. In a medium sauté pan, add 6 Tbsp. butter and add coated chicken. Grill on both sides until both sides are golden brown. Put on plate, then add 1 slice of the Provolone cheese on top of the chicken breast. Cover with the glaze sauce.

Submitted by Les Williams, kitchen manager

SUGAR MOUNTAIN

2396 N. College Ave
Fayetteville AR 72703
(479) 443-9500
sugarmtnroadhouse@yahoo.com

Sugar Mountain Roadhouse was originally established as a restaurant and gallery in which the owners featured some local artists work as well as some well known prints for sale. In September of 2005, changes were made, in management, food and atmosphere. Changes continued to present day July, 2006. The restaurant and gallery has now become a roadhouse bar and refined dining establishment. As a local journalist described, "rough and refined", (Arkansas Democrat Gazette, June 2006).

The restaurant/soda fountain serves Burgers, Barbeque and Steaks as well as a full array of fountain treats. The bar features nightly drink specials, Texas Hold'em Poker and Karaoke two nights a week. Sugar Mountain Roadhouse is a fun place to go for a nice dinner or just plain ol' fun at the bar. Located in Fayetteville, Arkansas on the corner of Township and College (71B), you can't miss it. So whenever you are in the area, drop on in, we will be glad to serve you some really good barbeque and fun.

Drunk Chicken

1 qt. beer–any kind
1 regular size 'Wish Bone' Italian dressing–no substitute
1 stick butter
1-2 whole chickens or the equivalent in chicken pieces

Directions

Melt butter in large pan, add Italian dressing and beer. Cut up chicken, add to the pot and simmer all of this for about 15 minutes. Remove the chicken from the mix and finish cooking on the grill–charcoal or gas, it doesn't matter. The alcohol content will cook out and the chicken will tender and tasty.

Serve with any of your favorite barbeque side dishes. The chicken is good cold, too.

Submitted by Tina St. John-Horner, manager

THE OL' ROCKHOUSE RESTAURANT

416 South Pine Street
Scenic Hwy. 7 South
Harrison, AR
(870) 741-8047

Located on scenic Hwy. 7 South, The Ol' Rockhouse is owned by husband and wife team Tracy and Dan Orr. All barbeque and prime rib is smoked on the premises. Home of the famous Rockhouse Burger. Open 11 a.m. to 9 p.m. and 11 a.m. to 3 p.m. on Sunday.

Herb Chicken
This is so special it is only on the menu certain times

½ chicken
½ tsp. tarragon
½ tsp. pepper
½ tsp. onion powder

½ tsp. rosemary
½ tsp. salt
½ tsp. garlic powder

Directions

Place chicken on large sheet tray. Evenly sprinkle all seasonings over chicken. Cover with foil and bake at 350° for 30 minutes. Uncover and bake until done.

This recipe can be adjusted to each person depending on how much seasoning an individual likes. We mix a big batch of seasoning up and use it to coat the chicken.

Submitted by Tracy & Dan Orr, owners

TOOTHPICKS CHOPHOUSE

324 W. Dickson St.
Fayetteville, AR 72701
(479) 521-6880

At Toothpicks we sell the finest meat money can buy and age the beef for 50 days before we serve it. We also slow smoke our BBQ meats for at least 12 hours with a dry rub. This is my favorite chicken recipe. I hope you enjoy.

Jerk Chicken

2 limes, 2 lemons, 2 oranges
1 habenero pepper
½ c. granulated garlic
1 Tbsp. Tyme
3 Tbsp. cinnamon
3 Tbsp. allspice
1 c. soy sauce
3 Tbsp. red pepper flakes
1½ c. apple cider vinegar

1 - 6 oz. can pineapple juice
1½ c. jalapenos
1 medium white onion
2 Tbsp. salt
3 Tbsp. ginger
3 Tbsp. nutmeg
1½ c. olive oil
2 c. brown sugar

Directions

Puree first eight ingredients in food processor. Then wisk in the rest of the ingredients. Makes 4 quarts of marinade. Marinade chicken breast for 4 hours then grill to done. Serve with whatever sides you like.

Submitted by chef Tim Freeman

RESTAURANT Recipes of

MISCELLANEOUS

ANGLERS WHITE RIVER RESORT

Intersection of Hwy. 5, 9 & 14 at Allison
Mountain View, AR 72560
(870) 585-2226
www.anglerswhiteriver.com

Located on the world famous White River, Anglers is a full service resort, offering lodging and dining overlooking the river in a casual sportsmen's atmosphere of domestic and exotic wildlife mounts. Anglers Dock offers guided trout fishing services, boats and motors, raft and canoe rentals.

Anglers Honey Mustard
Dressing & Dipping Sauce

1 gal. salad dressing
2 c. half and half
5 Tbsp. wine vinegar
1½ Tbsp. granulated garlic
½ Tbsp. white pepper

2 c. honey
¼ c. prepared mustard
5 Tbsp. lemon juice
1 Tbsp. salt

Directions

Mix salad dressing, honey, half and half, wine vinegar and lemon juice together. Mix remaining dry ingredients well and add to mixture. Stir until creamy.

Submitted by Susie Peceny, owner

APPLE CREST INN

**Apple Crest Inn
Bed and Breakfast**

**12758 South Highway 59
Gentry, AR 72734
(479) 736-8201 or 888-APPLE US
www.applecrestinn.com**

Located at the foot of the Ozarks between Siloam Springs and Gentry in a place the locals call "Sleepy Hollow," our Victorian home and carriage house offers guests old-world elegance complete with modern-day convenience. The area is well-known in Arkansas history as being a playground for the rich. President Hayes signed the first deed on the property where Apple Crest Inn stands. Today we specialize in English High Teas, Murder Mystery Dinners and special occasions.

Benedictine Croissant Casserole

10 eggs
1 c. mixed colby/cheddar cheese, shredded
1 tsp. dill seed
1 - 8 oz. cream cheese - diced small
1 pkg. G. Washington Golden seasoning
10 small or 5 large croissants
Hollandaise sauce

3 c. milk
½ c. pepperjack cheese - shredded
1 tsp. dill weed
1 tsp. ground mustard
1 onion diced and sauteed
10 slices wham (vegetarian ham)
Real ham slices can be used as well, but this makes a very nice vegetarian dish.

Directions

Make in either a 9x13" glass pan or in individual round baking dishes. Fill cups with half of torn croissants. Dice cream cheese into small cubes and place over croissants. Tear wham or ham slices up and place over cream cheese. Mix eggs, milk, dill seed, dill weed, cheese, mustard, seasonings and sauteed onion together. Pour mixture over the half filled dish. Add more croissants and rest of mixture. Top with the pepperjack cheese.

Bake in oven at 350° for one hour. Can be made the night before and placed in the refrigerator. Take out one hour before baking time is started. Take out of baking container and serve with Hollandaise sauce over top.

Submitted by Dianne and Gary Affolter, owners

BEAN PALACE RESTAURANT

War Eagle Mill
11045 War Eagle Rd.
Rogers, AR 72756
(479) 789-5343

A water-powered Grist Mill
Rogers, Arkansas

Bean Palace Restaurant specializes in fresh ground cornmeal and buckwheat flour to serve cornbread, biscuits, buckwheat waffles and home homemade bread for sandwiches. Housed on the third floor of a working water-powered grist mill, War Eagle Mill on the War Eagle River.

War Eagle Cornbread

1¾ c. cornmeal
¾ c. unbleached or whole wheat flour
1 Tbsp. baking powder
½ tsp. salt

1½ c. milk
1 egg
2 Tbsp. honey
1 Tbsp. butter or margarine

Directions

Preheat a 10-inch cast-iron skillet in a 375° oven. If using a baking pan, no need to preheat – size should be 9 x 11 inch. Combine liquid ingredients; add to dry. Stir well. Coat with butter. Pour batter into pan. Bake for about 25-30 minutes or until golden brown. A feast for 4 hungry people.

War Eagle Buttermilk Biscuits

1c. white whole wheat flour
1 c. all-purpose flour
1 Tbsp. baking powder
½ tsp. baking soda

4 Tbsp. shortening
1 c. buttermilk
½ tsp. salt

Directions

Preheat oven to 475°. Cut shortening into flour, salt, baking powder, and soda with pastry cutter or using your fingers until mixture looks like coarse meal. Stir in the buttermilk. Turn out on floured board, folding once. Roll out and cut biscuits. Bake on cookie sheet with biscuits touching one another or in a 9 x 11-inch baking pan for about 12 minutes. Save your biscuit cuttings and roll into a rectangle, sprinkle with cinnamon and sugar. Roll lengthwise and cut into ½" pieces for bite size kid pleasers.

Submitted by Zoe Caywood, milleress emeritus

BLUFF STEAKHOUSE AT BIGGER'S BED & BREAKFAST

Overlooking the Spring River

20 Bluff Rd.
Hardy, AR 72542
(870) 856-4718
www.biggersbnb.com

At Bigger's Bed & Breakfast Bluff Steakhouse we create a homey atmosphere with casual fine dining. Our customers are our best advertisers. If you're looking for great food – look no further.

Sundried Tomato Focaccia

1 pkg. yeast
2 c. and 2 Tbsp. all-purpose flour
1 tsp. salt

1 c. lukewarm water
2 Tbsp. whole wheat flour

Toppings:
Stuffed tomatoes
Onions
Basil
Pepper

Artichokes
Garlic
Parsley

Directions

In a small bowl, mix dry yeast and water. Combine both flour and salt in food processor. With machine running add yeast mixture through feed tube. Pulse 30 times. Dough will be sticky. Let the dough rise till double, about 1 hour. Spray baking sheet with nonstick oil. Form dough into ball, press into 12" circle. Cover with plastic wrap and let rise for 30 minutes. Preheat oven to 425°. Make dimples all over dough with fingertips. Do not pierce. Cover with your choice of topping. Bake for 15-20 minutes or until browned.

Submitted by Valerie Bathrick, owner

BOTTINI'S RESTAURANT

103 W. Rush
Harrison, AR 72601
(870) 741-4511

Chef Nicholas Bottini is the artisan behind the fine cuisine at Bottini's Restaurant. He is a graduate of the Culinary Institute of America (CIA) in Hyde Park, New York. His Italian/Sicilian parents and grandparents instilled in him a love of fine food which he loves to share with others. His restaurant was featured in Southern Living.

Pasta Puttanesca

1 oz. basil
1 oz. capers
1 oz. shallots
1 oz. garlic
1 oz. sliced black olives

2 Tbsp. olive oil
6 oz. angel hair pasta, cooked
2 oz. white wine, 2 Tbsp. cold butter
1 oz. sun-dried tomatoes
2 fillets anchovies

Optional: crushed red pepper flakes, salt and pepper to taste

Directions

Sauté basil, capers, shallots, garlic, sun-dried tomatoes, black olives, anchovies in olive oil until garlic is light brown, add white wine and butter. Toss with angel hair pasta; plate and serve.

Submitted by Chef Nicholas Bottini

CIMARRON RESTAURANT

U.S. 62 & U.S. 412
Ash Flat, AR 72513
(870) 994-7776

This is a family owned restaurant which serves home cooked meals. We make all our soups from scratch. Specials everyday.

Squash Casserole

6 c. diced squash
Boil 5 minutes and drain.

½ c. diced onion

1 can cream of chicken soup
1 c. shredded carrots
Mix with squash

1 c. sour cream

1 pkg. Stove-top Stuffing Mix

1 stick butter

Directions

Melt butter, add stuffing. Put half of mix into squash mixture and put in baking dish. Add rest of stuffing mix on top of squash. Bake at 350° for 30 minutes.

Submitted by Carmen Goodman

DINO'S ITALIAN RESTAURANT

4628 Hwy. 62 East
Mountain Home, AR 72653
(870) 492-5080
dinositaliancuisine.com

In 1993 we opened Dino's Italian Restaurant in beautiful Mountain Home. The restaurant has a very relaxing atmosphere, soft music and decorated in fine Italian art. Great selection of fine dishes, wines, beers and desserts.

Pomodoro - Angel Hair

8 oz. Angel Hair in salted boiling water (all dente)

3 Tbsp. mild olive oil

1 clove garlic, minced

Handful fresh basil - julienne

1 c. fresh chopped tomatoes (not too small)

Salt and ground pepper

Directions

Heat oil, add garlic. Stir for a few seconds and add tomatoes and basil in medium heat, stirring a few minutes. Add salt and pepper and Angel Hair and some liquid from pasta or chicken stock. Toss well and serve. Can be topped with sautéd chicken tenders or shrimp.

Submitted by Eliana and Dino, chefs and owners

Elizabeth's Restaurant & Catering

231 East Main Street
Historic Downtown
Batesville, AR 72501
(870) 698-0903

Family-owned and operated, Elizabeth's Restaurant and Catering provides casual fine dining in a relaxed, friendly atmosphere. Located in the heart of historic downtown Batesville in the Hail Building (built in 1908) we're open for lunch Tuesday through Saturday 10:30 a.m. to 3 p.m. and dinner Thursday through Saturday from 5 p.m. to 9 p.m. A great dining experience!

Green Bean Bundles

1 - 32 oz. bag whole green beans, frozen
Salt
Garlic Salt
4 stick butter

23 strips bacon, cut in half
Pepper
1 - 1 lb. box light brown sugar

Directions

Thaw green beans. Place 5 or 6 green beans onto a half strip of bacon. Roll, the place in pan – seam side down. When pan is full, sprinkle bundles with salt, pepper and garlic powder. Melt 4 sticks of butter and mix with brown sugar. Cover pan with foil and bake at 350° for an hour or until bacon is crispy. Makes 15 servings of 3 bundles.

Submitted by Diane White, owner

JOJO'S CATFISH WHARF

6 miles north of Mtn. View on Hwy. 5
at Jack's White River Fishing Resort
Mountain View, AR 72560
(870) 585-2121

Jo Jo's Catfish Wharf was established in 1995. Located on the bank of the White River amid Jack's Fishing Resort, the restaurant offers scenic river view dining. The specialty of this family-oriented establishment is catfish fillets, however, one will find many other menu items that would delight anyone's taste buds.

Cheesy Potatoes

6 red potatoes, shredded
1 small onion, finely chopped
½ stick butter
Small amount of water

1 c. grated American cheese
White pepper
Seasoned pepper
Parsley flakes

Directions

Cook the shredded potatoes, onion, butter and water in skillet with lid until potatoes are tender. Then add cheese (more if preferred). Sprinkle cheese on top, allow to melt, then stir it into potatoes. Sprinkle with white pepper, seasoned pepper and parsley flakes and stir. (This also makes great cheese-potato soup by adding extra milk and water.)

Submitted by Jo & Mike Mitchell, owners

JOSIE'S STEAKHOUSE

50 Riverbank Dr.
Batesville, AR 72501
(870) 793-7000

Josie's Steakhouse began as an addition to a dairy bar and gas station in Waldenburg, AR in 2001. Named after the first granddaughter of proprietors Steve and Beth Carpenter, Josie's quickly became famous for providing the highest quality food in a fun, family focused atmosphere. In February of 2004, the Carpenter family brought their homemade flavor and down-home flair to Batesville, opening at the beautiful Lockhouse Restaurant overlooking the White River. Priding itself on providing the highest quality food possible, Josie's is one of only a few restaurants in Arkansas that serves hand-carved 100% Certified Angus Beef steaks, one of the highest quality meats on the market. From karaoke contests and out door dining to event catering and live concerts, Josie's aims to please by providing the place where good times are had, memories are made and everyone feels at home!

Josie's Fried Rice

2 c. white onions
1 c. celery
3 chicken breasts, cubed
3 large eggs
¼ c. sesame seeds
16 oz. teriyaki sauce

1 c. green onions
1 c. shredded carrots
9 shrimp, cubed
¼ c. pepper
¼ c. granulated garlic
20 oz. soy sauce

Directions

Get cooking surface hot and prep with olive oil. Place white onions, green onions, celery, carrots on the grill and mix together. On opposite side, add chicken and shrimp. Be sure to keep separate from vegetables. Add ¼ c. pepper, ¼ c. sesame seeds, ¼ c. granulated garlic to vegetables. When meat is cooked, add 3 eggs, also keeping separate from other ingredients. After combining the chopped eggs with meat and vegetables, add rice and mix. Add teriyaki and soy sauce, sesame seed and garlic to taste. Decrease to low heat and cook for 10 minutes, stirring occasionally. (No soy or teriyaki should remain on the grill)

Submitted by Dustin Carpenter, manager

MAMA Z's CAFE

357 W. Henri De Tonti Blvd.
Tontitown, AR 72770
(479) 361-2750
www.mamazs.net

Mama Z's opened in May 1988 accomplishing a life-long dream of Edna (Morsani) Zulpo to have a cafe using many old recipes handed down from Edna's Nonna (grandmother). Mama Z's serves breakfast, lunch and dinner offering homemade pastas, sauces, rolls and jellies.

Mama Z's Meat Sauce

¼ c. butter
2½ c. chopped onion
1¾ c. chopped celery
2 Tbsp. minced garlic
3 - 12 oz. cans tomato paste
3 - 10½ oz. cans tomato puree

1¼ lb. ground beef
1 Tbsp. pepper
1 Tbsp. salt
2 Tbsp. sugar
7-10 c. water

Directions

Sauté onion, celery and garlic in butter until clear. Add ground beef and cook until brown. Add salt, pepper, sugar, tomato paste and puree and 7 cups of water. Bring to a boil. Reduce heat and simmer on very low or in a crock pot for at least 4 hours, stirring occasionally.

Submitted by Yvonne Otwell, Mama Z's daughter

We'll Feed You Right

115 West Elm St.
Walnut Ridge, AR 72476
(870) 886-7521

Moni's Steakhouse & Grill is a home-owned and operated full-service restaurant. Featuring home style cooking at its finest. Breakfast available all day! Serving everything from breakfast through dinner including catfish handcut, char grill steaks, specialty salads, sandwiches and more. Open 7 days a week.

Mom's Cajun Steak & Eggs Benedict

1 English muffin
6 oz. diced sirloin steak
½ c. Hollandaise sauce

2 eggs
3 tsp. Cajun seasoning

Directions

Halve English muffin, lightly butter and grill. Poach eggs in egg poacher. Season steak with 2 tsp. Cajun and cook to desired wellness. Place halves of grilled English muffin on plate. Top with grilled Cajun steak (diced). Placed poached eggs on top of steak. Cover with heated Hollandaise sauce and sprinkle other tsp. of Cajun over sauce. Delicious! Serve with a side of hot, streaming hashbrowns.

Submitted by Moni's Steakhouse & Grill staff

MORNINGSIDE COFFEE HOUSE

1006 St. Louis Street
Batesville, AR 72501
(870) 793-3335

Step into MorningSide Coffee House and sit down to enjoy a little slice ofthe city life in the small town of Batesville, AR. Our funky atmosphere is complimented with a friendly staff that takes our coffee quality seriously, while offering up a wide selection of delectable homemade desserts, fresh deli sandwiches, bagels and soup. We are well known for our fresh hot scones and muffins each morning so come early or call ahead! *Call us for your catering and/or party needs.

Biscotti di Prato

¾ c. whole almonds
3 eggs
1 tsp. vanilla
¼ tsp. almond extract

2 c. flour
⅞ c. sugar
1 tsp. baking soda
Dash of salt

Directions

Place nuts in a shallow pan and bake in pre-heated 350° over for 8-10 minutes or until golden brown. Let cool. In small bowl, beat eggs, vanilla and almond extract with a wire whisk. In a mixing bowl combine flour, sugar, baking soda and salt. Add egg mixture and mix until blended, about 1 minute. Cut nuts into halves or thirds and mix in. Divide dough in half on a greased and floured baking sheet. Pat out dough into 2 logs about ½" thick, 1½" wide and 12" long, spaced at least 2" apart. Bake in middle of pre-heated 300° oven for 50 minutes or until golden brown. Let cool on pan or wire rack. Place on a cutting board and cut slices with a serrated knife on a 45 degree angle about ½" thick. Lay the slices flat on the baking sheet and return to a 275° oven for 20-25 minutes or until toasted, turning them over once about halfway during the baking time. Store in a tightly covered container.

Enjoy by dipping into your favorite strong cup of coffee or Italian red wine.

Submitted by Dani Kvern, owner

Other Books From The Publisher

Restaurant Recipes
of Kansas City

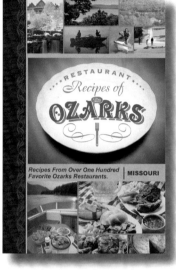

Restaurant Recipes
of the Ozarks

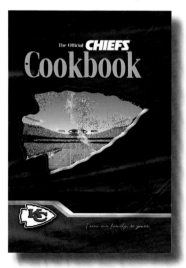

The Kansas City
Chiefs Cookbook

To Order Call:
(800) 313-5121

OZARK MOUNTAIN SMOKE HOUSE

Farmington, AR 72730
(800) 643-3437

In 1946 a small smokehouse was built by Roy Sharp and the Ozark Mountain Smoke House was launched as a business/hobby(?). In 1962 Roy's son, Frank, and his wife, Sara, became actively involved in the business, which they still operate (with their four children) on the Sharp farm on the slopes of Mount Kessler. Visitors are cordially invited to visit Mount Kessler and the smokehouse and kitchens of the Ozark Mountain Family.

Farmer's Breakfast

1 small onion, chopped
⅓ c. chopped green sweet pepper
1 c. chopped smoked ham

6 eggs slightly beaten
½ c. milk
Tabasco to taste

Sauté onions, green pepper and ham in 3 Tbsp. butter n large skillet. Mix eggs, milk and seasoning and pour into skillet. Scramble gently two or three minutes until set. Good with hot biscuits.

Best Ever Ham Loaf

1 lb. ground veal
1 lb. ground smoked ham
4 Tbsp. catsup
2 Tbsp. minced onion
3 Tbsp. chopped green pepper
2 eggs, beaten

1 c. dry bread crumbs
1 can condensed cream of mushroom soup
¼ c. water
½ tsp. salt
Dash of pepper

Mix together in order given, pack into greased loaf pan and bake in moderate oven (350°) for 1 hour. Serves 8. Serve hot or cold, preferably with mustard sauce.

Hot Stuff Mustard Sauce

1 egg, well beaten
1 Tbsp. sugar
¼ tsp. salt

3 Tbsp. dry mustard
½ c. white vinegar
1 Tbsp. olive oil

Mix egg, sugar, salt, mustard (yes, 3 Tbsp. is right) and vinegar in top of double boiler, and cook, stirring until thick. Cook, then stir in the oil. Serve with cold or hot meats.

Submitted by Ozark Mountain Family Cookbook

RIVER GRILLE STEAKHOUSE

STEAKHOUSE

1003 McClain Road
Bentonville, AR 72712
(479) 271-4141

Touted as one of the state's finest restaurants by local newspaper readers, the River Grille is an experience for the senses! The menu features center of the plate hand-cut U.S.D.A. prime aged beef and fresh fish flown in daily. Creative and exciting daily special prepared by talented chefs and an extensive wine list of over 200 bottles of fines wines, which has received the Award of Excellence from Wine Spectator for five consecutive years.

Yellow Fin Tuna Crab & Potato Cakes

3 eggs
2 Tbsp. Dijon mustard
1 c. minced green onion (not packed)
2 50 cnt. par cooked Idaho potato
  peeled & shredded
1 Tbsp. old bay
3 dashes Tabasco
1 Tbsp. Worcestershire
1½ c. mayo or more as needed
Juice of 2 lemons
½ c. chopped Italian parsley
2 tsp. celery seed
1 tsp. 5 peppercorn mélange
1 Tbsp. lemon pepper
1 tsp. garam masala
1 Tbsp. garlic powder
2 c. ground Japanese bread crumbs or more as needed
2 lbs. Janna Tuna loin, drained
2 lbs. lump crab, drained

Directions

Combine & mix well all ingredients except bread crumbs.

When ingredients are thoroughly mixed start incorporating bread crumbs kneading with hands so that it will hold together and a test cake will hold up in fryer.

Form into three ½ oz. patties (2 per order)

Submitted by Brenda Swango, owner

RiverSide Kitchen

2 Frost Street
Gilbert, AR 72636
(870) 439-2288

Next to the Buffalo River and the small town of Gilbert, AR is where you will find the Award Winning RiverSide Kitchen, where anyone who comes in, is a stranger for a minute, and family from then on. With foods made from scratch...huge yeast rolls, decadent fudge cake, bread pudding and fresh baked cinnamon rolls...to an almost endless variety of main entrees from fried catfish with real mashed potatoes and gravy, smoked meats, Mexican food, full pound burger or a juicy ribeye. RiverSide is a regular stop for those traveling to and from Eureka Springs and Branson and now does catering for private and corporate events.

Homemade Maple Syrup

Most folks don't realize that you can make your syrup for waffles and pancakes.
You can also add blueberry, strawberry or any flavoring you like.

6 c. water   12 c. sugar
3 tsp. maple flavoring

Directions

Bring water to a boil, add sugar and flavoring. Boil 2 minutes stirring constantly. Remove from heat and serve warm. Store in refrigerator tightly covered. This will make 6 cups of syrup.

Brown Sugar Syrup (low fat)

2 c. packed light brown sugar   1 c. water

Directions

Bring sugar and water to a boil over medium heat stirring constantly. Boil 5 minutes and serve warm. Store in refrigerator.

Submitted by Jill Hackett, owner

SODIE'S FOUNTAIN & GRILL

Flippin Depot
Junction US Hwy 62/412 and AR Hwy 178
109 N. First Street
Flippin, Arkansas 72634
(870) 453-7632
www.sodies.com

Sodie's Fountain & Grill is located in a recreated turn of the century train station. Complete with antique soda fountain, mirrored back bar, and 20-foot marble counter, Sodie's will take you back to a time when the corner drug store was the town's gathering place. Sodie's serves an extensive, homemade, breakfast, lunch and dinner menu, along with all your favorite ice cream treats. There is also a big gift shop, patio seating, and meeting room. Bus and RV parking is available in the rear of the building. Sodie's is open daily except Thanksgiving, Christmas and New Year's.

Maureen's Mexican Rice

4 c. cooked rice, according to the package directions plus 1 Tbsp. salt
1 lb. Monterey Jack cheese, sliced or shredded

2 c. sour cream
2 cans Ortega Green Chili's, split open and seeds removed

Directions

Grease 3 qt. casserole dish. Mix rice and sour cream together. Put approximately 1 inch deep layer of rice mixture in bottom of dish. Cover with a layer of chilies, then a layer of cheese. Repeat until rice mixture is used up, ending with a layer of cheese.

Bake at 350° until heated through and cheese is melted. This can also be microwaved. Use half power and turn often.

Submitted by Gary & Maureen Fancher

SPICE O'LIFE BAKERY/CAFE

"The Natural Tastes of Arkansas"
200 N. Spring St.
Jasper, AR 72641
(870) 446-2468

Since 1993 we have lived up to our byline, "The Natural Taste of Arkansas," by using locally grown produce and even naturally occurring fruits and berries as available. We serve deli-style lunch Tuesday through Friday and pizza and pasta on Friday and Saturday nights. We make pastries and special occasion cakes. We also bake bread and cookies for both retail and wholesale markets.

Tomato Cream Sauce

1 c. chopped onion
2 Tbsp. olive oil
1 - 12 oz. can tomato paste
3 tsp. dried oregano, crushed
¼ tsp. black pepper
¼ c. vodka (optional)
1 lb. Fettuccine, cooked

4 tsp. minced garlic
4 - 14½ oz. cans Italian-style stewed
 tomatoes, undrained and cut up
½ tsp. salt
1 c. whipping cream
½ c. snipped fresh flat-leaf parsley

Directions

In a large saucepan, cook and stir onion over medium heat until onion is tender. Add garlic, undrained tomatoes, tomato paste, oregano, salt and pepper. Bring to a boil, reduce heat and simmer, uncovered about 10 minutes, stirring occasionally. Slowly add the cream and vodka, stirring the mixture constantly. Cook and stir for 3 more minutes. remove from heat and stir in parsley. Serve over hot cooked pasta.

Submitted by Leon and Jan Doud, owners

540 Sidney St.
St. James, MO 65559
(800) 280-9463
www.StJamesWinery.com

St. James Winery is owned and operated by the Hofherr Family since 1970, conveniently located on Interstate 44, on Old Historic Route 66 only ninety miles southwest of St. Louis, Missouri in St. James, Missouri .

With over 700 miles of vines in Missouri, Arkansas, and Michigan, no other winery in the Eastern United states utilizes such state of the art technology from the vineyards to the bottling room bringing you consistent quality vintages for your enjoyment. With over 1,800 medals to date, no wonder St. James Winery is "America's Midwest Winery". In our area, be sure to stop by our tasting room and sample our wide variety of vintages, our extensive gift shop, and take a tour of our cellars. St. James Winery products are presently distributed in six states and available on our website.

Bow Tie Pasta with Asparagus and Shrimp

1 lb. bow tie pasta

1 lb. fresh asparagus

3 Tbsp. of corn starch

4 Tbsp. of butter

1 lb. of peeled and de veined shrimp

2 Tbsp. fresh chopped parsley (optional)

2-3 tsp. of Extra Virgin Olive Oil

1 c. of St. James Winery Chardonel

½ to ⅓ c. grated Romano cheese to taste

3- 4 Tbsp. of fresh crushed garlic to taste

1 c. whipping cream

Salt and fresh ground pepper to taste

Directions

Cook pasta, drain and set aside. In medium sauce pan, sauté shrimp in two tablespoons of butter and 2 tablespoons of fresh crushed garlic. Stir in asparagus and sauté until al dente. Set aside

Heat the remaining 2 tablespoons of butter with the olive oil and garlic. Stir in St. James Chardonel and over medium heat stirring, reduce liquid to half the amount, then add cream and cornstarch. Whisk over low heat until thickened.

Add drained pasta, shrimp, and asparagus into the sauce stirring mixture together, add grated cheese and parsley. Serve in large pasta bowl and garnish with parsley leaves. Serves 6.

Submitted by Jack Bonar

THE FEED STORE CAFE

THE FEED STORE CAFE
GENTRY, ARKANSAS

136 S. Gentry Blvd.
Gentry, AR 72734
(479) 736-3481

The Feed Store Cafe is located in Gentry, AR. It is owned by Herb and Pat Varner. It has been owned, operated and in the same location for almost 12 years. The Feed Store Cafe has excellent homemade food, friendly staff and wonderful small town charm. Y'all come and see us!

Sara's Country Scramble

1 c. has browns
1 bell pepper, chopped
¼ c. shredded cheddar cheese

1 med. onion, white or yellow, chopped
2 eggs, scrambled
½ c. white gravy

Directions

Grill one order of hash browns. Sauté onions and bell peppers and add to hash browns. Top with shredded cheddar cheese, 2 scrambled eggs and white gravy. Serve with your choice of toast or biscuit. This recipe can be added to easily serve more people.

Submitted by Herb & Pat Varner, owner

1400 Central Blvd.
Bull Shoals, AR 72619
(870) 445-4414

The Village Wheel Restaurant, located in beautiful Bull Shoals, AR has been family-owned for 24 years, serving breakfast, lunch and dinner 7 days a week. Owners Cindy Crosslin and Danette Stubenfoll opened a gift shop in March 2005 which has unique gifts for that hard-to-buy-for person. The Village Wheel Restaurant specializes in Broasted Chicken. Monday nights is all you can eat chicken. Wednesday nights feature Canadian Walleye, Thursday nights feature quail, Friday nights has all you can eat popcorn shrimp or Alaskan white fish and Saturday nights offer prime rib. Skillet breakfasts have also been added to the menu. There is a private dining room for banquets and regular customers enjoy our birthday and anniversary club.

Firehouse Beans

1 - 29 oz. can bush baked beans
  drained & rinsed
1 - 15 oz. can dark kidney beans,
  drained & rinsed

1 - 15 oz. can butter beans, drained & rinsed
1 - 15 oz. can lima beans, drained & rinsed
2 medium onions, sliced
1 lb. ground chuck, fried & drained well (opt.)

Put all above ingredients in a 9 x 13 inch pan. Mix well.

Sauce:
½ lb. bacon, diced & fried crisp (1 lb.)
Drain off ½ of the grease
1¼ c. brown sugar (2½ c.)
5 oz. catsup (1¼ c.)

3 oz. cider vinegar (¾ c.)
½ tsp. salt (1 tsp.)
1 tsp. dry mustard (2 tsp.)

Directions

Fry bacon and drain half the grease. Add the rest of the ingredients and mix well. Let sauce come to a slow boil. Add to beans. Bake 1-2 hours at 350° stirring occasionally. The longer they bake the darker and thicker they become. They will also be thicker as they cool. Double sauce recipe ingredients are in parentheses.

Note: If you need a bigger batch you can triple the beans and still just double the sauce.

Submitted by Cindy & Danette, owners

RESTAURANT *Recipes of* DESSERTS

101's GREAT AMERICAN DINER

3414 Hwy. 101
Gamaliel, AR 72537
(870) 467-5126

A comfortable country atmosphere featuring lots of country and kitchen antiques. We offer awesome home cooking with breakfast served all day with mouth watering omelettes and pancakes that overflow the plates. Nestled in the wonderful resort area of Lake Norfork, we are within walking distance from campgrounds and cabins and just minutes from crystal clear Lake Norfork.

Iron Skillet Pineapple Upside Down Cake

¼ c. butter or margarine
½ c. chopped pecans
3 eggs, separated
1 c. all-purpose flour
½ tsp. salt
6-8 maraschino cherries

1 c. firmly packed brown sugar
1 (15 oz.) can pineapple slices
1 c. sugar
1 tsp. baking powder

Directions

Melt butter in a 9" cast iron skillet. Add brown sugar and pecans, stir well. Drain pineapple. Reserve ¼ c. of the juice; set juice aside. Arrange pineapple slices in a single layer over brown sugar mixture. Set skillet aside. Beat egg yolks at medium speed with electric mixer until thick and lemon colored. Gradually add sugar, beating well. Combine flour, baking powder and salt. Add dry mixture to yolk mixture, stir in reserved pineapple juice. Beat egg whites until stiff peaks form. Fold whites into batter. Spread evenly over pineapple slices. Bake at 350° for 40-45 minutes. Cool cake in skillet for 30 minutes. Invert onto serving plate. Place cherries in center of pineapple rings.

Submitted by Tina Montgomery, chef/owner

178 CLUB RESTAURANT

2109 Central Blvd.
Bull Shoals, AR 72618
(870) 445-4949
www.178club.com

We pride ourselves in maintaining the highest standard of quality and excellence so common fifty years ago, but so rare today. We are family owned and operated and are proud to have been at this same location in Bull Shoals for over 26 years. We prepare your meal when you place your order, using only the highest quality and freshest ingredients to ensure your dining pleasure. You see, we are not resting on a reputation; we're building one!

Rhubarb Pudding Cake

This is one of our most requested desserts.

Cake:

1 c. granulated sugar
2 Tbsp. melted butter or margarine
½ tsp. salt
1 tsp. baking powder
1 c. rhubarb

1 egg
1 c. buttermilk or sour milk
½ tsp. baking soda
2 c. all-purpose flour

Topping:

2 Tbsp. melted margarine

½ c. granulated sugar

Vanilla Sauce:

1 c. granulated sugar
½ c. evaporated milk

½ c. margarine
1 tsp. vanilla

Directions

Blend together sugar, egg and butter and beat in buttermilk until smooth. Stir together salt, baking soda, baking powder and flour then stir dry ingredients into buttermilk mixture. Mix well. Stir in rhubarb. Pour into a greased 9" or sheet pan. Combine topping ingredients and sprinkle on top of batter. Bake at 350° for 45 minutes or until cake is done. For sauce, mix sugar, margarine and milk. Bring to a boil and cook for one minute, stirring constantly. Remove from heat, stir in vanilla. Serve sauce over cake.

Submitted by the Fox family

APPLE CREST INN

Apple Crest Inn
Bed and Breakfast

12758 South Highway 59
Gentry, AR 72734
(479) 736-8201 or 888-APPLE US
www.applecrestinn.com

Located at the foot of the Ozarks between Siloam Springs and Gentry in a place the locals call "Sleepy Hollow," our Victorian home and carriage house offers guests old-world elegance complete with modern-day convenience. The area is well-known in Arkansas history as being a playground for the rich. President Hayes signed the first deed on the property where Apple Crest Inn stands. Today we specialize in English High Teas, Murder Mystery Dinners and special occasions.

English Lemon Scones

2 c. all-purpose flour
2 tsp. baking powder
¼ tsp. soda
⅓ c. butter or margarine
½ c. buttermilk (or sour milk -- fresh
  milk with lemon juice added)
1 Tbsp. milk

¼ c. sugar
1 tsp. finely shredded lemon peel - zest
¼ tsp. salt
1 beaten egg
2 tsp. sugar
Finely shredded lemon peel from 1 lemon

Directions

Stir together flour, ¼ c. sugar, baking powder, 1 tsp. lemon peel, baking soda, and salt. Using a pastry blender, cut in butter or margarine until mixture resembles coarse crumbs. Make a well in the center of dry mixture. Set aside. In another bowl, combine egg, and ½ c. buttermilk or sour milk. Add wet mixture all at one time to dry mixture. Using a fork, stir until moistened.

Turn dough out onto a lightly floured surface. Quickly knead dough for 10-20 strokes or until dough is nearly smooth. Pat dough into a 7 inch circle. Cut into 12 wedges or use round cutter. Place wedges or circles 1 inch apart on an ungreased baking sheet.

Combine 2 tsp. sugar and the rest of lemon peel. Brush wedges with 1 Tbsp. milk and sprinkle with sugar mixture. Bake in a 400° oven about 12 minutes or until golden. Remove from baking sheet and cool on a wire rack for 5 minutes. Serve warm. Makes 12 scones.

Submitted by Dianne and Gary Affolter, owners

Autumn Breeze
Restaurant

A Dining Pleasure

Hwy. 23 South
(½ mile off Hwy. 62)
Eureka Springs, AR 72362
(479) 253-7734
www.autumnbreezerestaurant.com

A fine dining steak and seafood house, Autumn Breeze boasts excellent food and a world class wine list presented professionally in an elegant dining room with a beautiful view. Lovely gardening and plenty of parking round out the experience. European born Chef Richard Bloch's specialities include: Coconut Beer Battered Shrimp, Rack of Lamb, New York Strip Peppercorn, Coquille St. Jacques, Veal Olympic and Chocolate Soufflés. Come see why the *Arkansas Times* declares, "Autumn Breeze Will Blow You Away."

Autumn Breeze Strawberry Pie

Pie Crust:

¼ lb. butter (salted)
½ c. cold water

1½ c. flour

Directions

Preheat oven to 450°F. Let butter soften at room temperature for 20 minutes. Cut butter in ¼ to ½ inch cubes. Add flour to butter, mix with a fork (or in a mixer with a dough hook, or use a food processor) until butter is in large pea sized pieces. Then add water slowly. When dough comes together, stop. Form the dough into a ball, let rest for 20 minutes. Roll out to ¼" thickness – this should result in a disk slightly larger than the diameter of the pan plus the sides. Place dough in the pan leaving a ½" hang over. Tuck the hang over under itself and flute decoratively with fingers. Prick bottom of the crust thoroughly with a fork. Place in preheated oven, bake for 12-15 minutes or until golden. Allow pie crust to cool 15 minutes before adding the filling.

Pie Filling:

4 pts. of strawberries
2 c. sugar
⅓ c. lemon juice

1¼ c. corn starch
1½ c. tap water

Directions

In a sauce pan mix water, sugar, lemon juice and starch. Stir until sugar and lemon juice are dissolved. Then put on stove on high heat, stirring continuously until the mixture is completely thickened. Add whole cleaned strawberries with the heat still on high. Slowly stir-in the berries until the starch turns red, approximately 2-3 minutes. Do not leave on heat too long. Spoon into prebaked, cooled, pie crust, spread evenly. Do not bake. Allow to set up for 3-4 hours at room temperature or in refrigerator for 2 hours. Serve!

Submitted by Chef Richard Bloch

BEAN PALACE RESTAURANT

War Eagle Mill
11045 War Eagle Rd.
Rogers, AR 72756
(479) 789-5343

Bean Palace Restaurant specializes in fresh ground cornmeal and buckwheat flour to serve cornbread, biscuits, buckwheat waffles and home homemade bread for sandwiches. Housed on the third floor of a working water-powered grist mill, War Eagle Mill on the War Eagle River.

Carrot Cake

2 c. sifted whole wheat flour
1 tsp. baking powder
2 tsp. baking soda
2 tsp. cinnamon
1 tsp. salt

¼ c. vegetable oil
2 c. finely grated carrots
3 eggs
1 - 15 oz. can crushed pineapple
¾ c. sugar

Directions

Sift together dry ingredients. Add oil, pineapple, carrots and eggs, one at a time. Mix well. Spread in 2 well-greased and floured round cake pans or an 11 x 13-inch baking pan.

Bake 35 minutes in a preheated 350° oven. Cool on racks in pans. Turn out on cake plate, frost top. Place other cake on top and frost. If using a single baking pan, do not turn out; let cool and frost.

Submitted by Zoe Caywood, milleress emeritus

BILL'S HICKORY HOUSE

1919 W. Sunset
Springdale, AR 72762
(479) 756-9886

Bill's Hickory House is a casual dining restaurant and full-service caterer, proudly serving our community for over 23 years.

Homemade Cobbler

2¼ c. sugar
2½ c. milk
2 Tbsp. baking powder
1 Tbsp. cinnamon
1½ c. juice from fruit (ow water)

3 c. flour (packed)
1 Tbsp. vanilla
1 tsp. salt
4 c. of your favorite fruit in heavy syrup
(or add ¼ c. sugar and ½ c. water to fresh fruit to make syrup)

Directions

In a bowl, combine sugar, flour, baking powder, salt and cinnamon. Mix well. Add vanilla and milk. Beat with wire whip until smooth. No lumps. Pour into greased 13.9 inch pan. Evenly spread fruit and juice over dough. Place in oven at 350° for 1½ to 2 hours or until center has fluffy breadlike consistency.

Submitted by Todd Spain, owner

Overlooking the Spring River

20 Bluff Rd.
Hardy, AR 72542
(870) 856-4718
www.biggersbnb.com

At Bigger's Bed & Breakfast Bluff Steakhouse we create a homey atmosphere with casual fine dining. Our customers are our best advertisers. If you're looking for great food – look no further.

Valerie's Dump Dessert
Everyone's favorite

9 x 12 cake pan
1 can apple pie filling
2 sticks butter, grated on top
⅔ c. brown sugar, sprinkle on top

1 can cherry pie filling
1 box yellow cake mix
1 c. oatmeal, sprinkle on top
1 tsp. cinnamon

Directions

Pour apple and cherry pie filling on the bottom. Then sprinkle cake mix evenly on top. Add rest of ingredients. Bake for 45 minutes at 350° until top is golden brown. Variation: any combination of 2 blueberries with apples, peaches or cherries.

Submitted by Valerie Bathrick, owner

BOI DE OURO BRAZILIAN STEAK HOUSE

741 East Van Asche
Fayetteville, AR 72703
(479) 521-1606

"Come to enjoy the complete Brazilian experience as gauchos continuously serve our many choices of prime meats, including steak, pork, lamb, chicken and sausage. We also have a salad bar with your meal that has many unique dishes found only at Boi de Ouro."

Brasilian Lime Mousse

700 ml heavy cream
600 ml fresh lime juice
1 tsp. green lime skin (no white)

700 ml. sweetened condensed milk
8 egg whites

Directions

Put 8 egg whites into mixing bowl and mix on high speed until stiff foam and peaks are formed.

In blender put heavy cream and sweetened condensed milk. Blend extremely well for 2 to 3 minutes. Add fresh lime juice and blend for 1 minute more. Add mixture from blender into the mixing bowl along with green (no white) skim from lime and mix for 2 to 3 minutes. Put into refrigerator for 3½ to 4 hours. Serves 12.

Submitted by Orlando Veronezi, general manager

BRENT'S RIB HOUSE & CATERING

400 Highway 201 North
Mountain Home, AR 72653
(870) 425-8080

Brent's Rib House & Catering opened September 7, 1997, in Mountain Home, Arkansas. Brent's features quick-serve barbecue with side orders and fruit cobblers of the day. Regarded as the best barbecue in the Twin Lakes area, Brent's is also the number one caterer in the area. They have catered food for groups as small as 20 people, and as large as 6000 people. Stop by Brent's Rib House for the best barbecue around.

German Chocolate Cookies

1 c. butter, softened
2 eggs
4 squares (1 oz. ea.) unsweetened chocolate
2¼ c. all-purpose flour
1 tsp. salt
½ c. coconut

2 c. sugar

2 tsp.s vanilla extract
1 tsp. baking soda
1 c. semisweet chocolate chips
½ c. pecans, chopped

Directions

Melt chocolate squares and cool slightly. In a mixing bowl, cream butter and sugar. Add eggs, one at a time, beating well after each addition. Beat in chocolate and vanilla. Combine the flour, baking soda, and salt; gradually add to the creamed mixture. Stir in chocolate chips, coconut, and pecans. Drop by tablespoonfuls 2 inches apart onto ungreased baking sheets. Bake at 375 degrees for 10-12 minutes or until tops are cracked. Remove to wire racks to cool. Yield: 4 dozen.

Submitted by Brent Smith, owner

BROWN'S DELTA BBQ & CATFISH

4007 Hwy. 67 South
Pocahontas, AR 72445
(870) 892-0142

Husband and wife team with a group of dedicated employees located 2 miles south of town. Hand rubbed pork spareribs served dry or wet. Catfish–fried or Cajun grilled served with the best hush puppies ever to touch human tongues.

Strawberry Pie

Baked pie crust
1 c. sugar
½ c. water

1½ qts. of strawberries
3 Tbsp. cornstarch
1 pkg. (3 oz.) cream cheese, soft

Directions

Mash enough strawberries to measure 1 cup. Mix sugar and cornstarch in 2 qt. sauce pan. Gradually stir in water and mashed strawberries. Cook on medium heat, stirring constantly until boiling and it thickens. Cook 1 minutes longer, let cool. Beat cream cheese until smooth. Spread cream cheese in bottom of pie shell. Fill shell with uncooked strawberries then pour cooked mixture over the top. Refrigerate about 3 hours until set. Top with whipped cream if desired.

Submitted by Lynn and John Brown, owners

CLIFF HOUSE INN

"Arkansas' Grandest View"
Scenic Highway 7 South
Jasper, AR 72641
(870) 446-2292
www.mcrush.com/cliffhouse

The Cliff House Inn has been written up as an "out of the ordinary, out of the way place." The dining room and our 5 unit motel has a spectacular view of the Arkansas Grand Canyon, the deepest canyon in Arkansas. The Cliff House Inn has been in operation since 1967, serving wonderful home cooking, along with a variety of delicious items on our menu. All of our desserts are homemade. We are famous for our Company's Comin' Pie, and Angel Flake Biscuits. The Cliff House Inn is located 6 miles south of Jasper, AR on scenic Highway 7.

Blackberry Cobbler

Melt:
  1 stick margarine

Make a batter of:
  1 c. flour   1 c. sugar
  1½ tsp. baking powder   1 c. milk

  2 cups blackberries

Directions

Pour batter into baking dish of melted butter. Do not stir. Pour 2 cups blackberries in to center of batter. Add 3 cups water or juice. Do not stir. If blackberries are unsweetened, sprinkle ½ cup sugar over them. Do not stir. Bake 45 minutes in over at 375˚.

Variations: Substitute blackberries with fresh or canned apples, peaches, cherries with 1 tsp. almond extract, or frozen strawberries.

How could anything so easy be so good? Season after season, cobbler is a favorite at the Cliff House Inn. Use fresh fruit or canned.

Submitted by Becky McLaurin

301 Southridge Blvd.
Heber Springs, AR 72543
(501) 362-5712

Cowboy Club House will tickle anyones taste buds. We offer Daily Lunch Specials, Home Cookin', BBQ, and really healthy menu items for those that want to tighten the ol' belt buckle. We also offer Blue Bell ice cream, old fashioned shakes, and homemade pies for dessert. Not only do we offer a, Kiss Your Grandma, good lunch but we serve breakfast on the weekends and breakfast all day on Sunday. So ya'll saddle up your horsepower and come on in, we look forward to seeing ya.

Peanut Butter Pie

8-12 oz. jar of creamy peanut butter
1¼ c. powdered sugar
1 Graham cracker crust (or Oreo crust)

8 oz. pkg. of cream cheese
2 c. heavy whipping cream

Directions

Mix together the peanut butter, cream cheese and ½ cup powdered sugar. In a separate bowl whip (high speed hand mixer) heavy whipping cream and the rest of the powdered sugar until soft peaks form. Stir in half of whipped cream into the peanut butter mixture until smooth and fold in the other half of whipped cream. Pour into graham cracker crust and refrigerate.

These pies can be frozen.

Submitted by Ashley Blankenship, owner

103 Historic Main Street
Calico Rock, AR
(870) 297-8899
www.donquixotes.net

Housed in the original Grocery Store Building on Calico Rock's historic Main Street by the White River, Don Quixote's has been open for business since 1996. Its 20-foot ceiling, hardwood floors, and straight back chairs take you back to the early 1900s.

The Berry Crisp

2 - 12 oz. pkgs. frozen mixed fruit
(blueberry, raspberry, blackberry)
½ c. Old Fashion Oats
½ c. butter

½ c. sugar
1 c. flour
⅔ c. brown sugar

Directions

Preheat oven 375° F. Combine berries, sugar and flour in a bowl. Toss Well. Make sure all of the berries are coated with the flour and sugar mixture. Transfer berry mixture into a 9 inch glass pie pan.

Take the remaining oats and sugar and put in bowl. Melt butter and add to mixture. Mix well. Top the berries in the glass bowl with the crunch not packing it into the berries.

Bake crisp until mixture bubbles thickly and topping is golden brown about 1 hour. Let stand 15 minutes. Serve warm.

Submitted by Gloria Gushue, owner

FOREST HILL RESTAURANT

Hwy. 62 E.
Next to Holiday Inn
Eureka Springs, AR 72632
(479) 253-2422
www.foresthillrestaurant.com

Opened in 1996 and located in historic Eureka Springs, AR, Forest Hill has always prided itself on pleasing the customer. With a variety of foods to choose from including choice steaks, an excellent buffet or wood burning oven pizzas, we have everything to fulfill your every need. We also have homemade desserts prepared in our own bakery! Be sure to drop by for a satisfying and enjoyable dining experience.

Chocolate Bourbon Pecan Pie

4 eggs
2 Tbsp. melted butter
1 tsp. vanilla
½ c. chocolate chips
1 - 10" pie crust

1 c. sugar
1 c. dark corn syrup
¼ c. bourbon
1 c. chopped pecan

Directions

Put chocolate chips and pecans in pie crust. Then combine eggs, sugar, melted butter, corn syrup, vanilla and bourbon and pour over the chocolate chips and pecans in the pie shell. Bake at 350° for 35-45 minutes for an excellent pecan pie.

Submitted by Mark Dewitz, baker

FRED'S HICKORY INN

"Keeping the Tradition Alive"
1502 N. Walton Blvd.
Bentonville, AR 72712
(479) 273-3303

Fred's Hickory Inn was started with the idea that "if we can serve quality food, offer good service and provide a comfortable atmosphere people will dine with us." Thirty-six years later we still slow smoke our meats on Fred's Original Smoker. We use the best quality meat available. Our steaks and chops are hand cut and grilled to perfection. And, of course, our spaghetti and cheesecake are Miss Lou's original recipe.

Sherry and the staff at Fred's are committed to keep the tradition that our founders and friends, Fred and Lou Gaye, started in 1970 alive for future generations.

Sherry's Old Fashioned Chocolate Cream Pie

1 baked pie shell
3 Tbsp. corn starch (heaping)
3 heaping Tbsp. Hershey's Cocoa
Dash of salt
2½ c. milk
1 tsp. vanilla

1 c. granulated sugar
3 egg yolks separated
  (Save whites for meringue)
½ c. hot tap water
1 Tbsp. butter

Directions

Mix all dry ingredients together in a heavy saucepan or on top of a double boiler. Whisk in hot water and egg yolks. Cook until thick and bubbly. Let boil at least 5 minutes while stirring. Be careful not to let it scorch. Take off the heat and add butter and vanilla. Let cool until at least room temperature. Pour in prepared pie shell.

Top with meringue or whipped crème.

To make meringue beat egg whites with dash of salt and 3 Tbsp. of sugar. Beat until it is very stiff and cover the top of your pie. Let brown in 350° oven.

Chocolate Whip Crème
2 c. heavy whipping crème
1 Tbsp. cocoa

4 Tbsp. powdered sugar
½ tsp. vanilla

Beat until stiff.

Submitted by Sherry Mendenhall, owner

HOMEY HEARTH BAKERY

905 N. Main
Harrison, AR 72601
(870) 741-4690

Homey Hearth Bakery has been voted #1 Bakery by Harrison consistently. Our goal is to provide top quality bakery and deli products in a relaxed Christian atmosphere. We are family owned and operated. Our dining room has seating for 40 and is soon to be expanded to hold 80-90 people.

Mini Cheese Cakes

These little cheesecakes are not only good, but are nice for parties or times when you are having finger foods.

12 vanilla wafers
½ c. sugar
1 tsp. vanilla

1 lb. cream cheese, softened
2 eggs
15 - ½ oz. can pie filling
(you choose flavor)

Directions
Mix cream cheese and sugar, add eggs and mix well. Add vanilla. Place a vanilla wafer in the bottom of cupcake papers and place in muffin tin. Divide filling between the 12. Should be about ¾ full. Bake at 325° for 20-25 minutes. Place a spoonful of fruit filling in center of each cheesecake.

Pumpkin Bread

This is a recipe we use in our bakery. Makes a good addition to breakfast or brunch. We have used this recipe from way back when we started the bakery in 1990.

3 c. sugar
1 c. oil
4 eggs
2 c. pumpkin
⅔ c. hot water
2 tsp. soda
3½ c. flour

½ tsp. baking powder
1 tsp. nutmeg
1 tsp. cloves
1 tsp. cinnamon
1½ tsp. salt
1 c. nuts

Directions
Mix sugar, oil and eggs and beat well. Add pumpkin and mix. Combine dry ingredients and add alternately with water. Place in two loaf pans (greased). bake at 350° for 1 hour or until done.

May glaze with powdered sugar icing made with powdered sugar and water.

Submitted by Clarence and Barb Yoder, owners

OZARK
RESTAURANT

Hwy. 5 & 9 North
Next to White River Hoedown
Mountain View, AR 72560
(870) 269-4136

Joshua's Ozark Restaurant was established in 1985 and has been a part of this small town ever since. We promote a family atmosphere with a friendly staff and home cooking just like mama used to do it. We have live music on the weekends, free of charge to anyone dining with us and large dining rooms for any of your family's needs or any other groups that need lots of seating. Groups of more than 20 please call for reservations.

Dirt Cake

1 large bag of Oreo cookies
8 oz. cream cheese
3½ c. milk
12 oz. container of Cool Whip

½ stick of butter
1 c. powdered sugar
1 large box of vanilla pudding

Directions

Break cookies up until finely crumbled in food processor. Blend cheese, butter and sugar in large bowl. Fold in Cool Whip. Mix pudding and milk in separate bowl. Layer cookies, then pudding mix, and then sugar mixture lasagna-style for 3 layers. Chill for 1 hour.

Submitted by Fred Hubbard, owner

MORNINGSIDE COFFEE HOUSE

1006 St. Louis Street
Batesville, AR 72501
(870) 793-3335

Step into MorningSide Coffee House and sit down to enjoy a little slice ofthe city life in the small town of Batesville, AR. Our funky atmosphere is complimented with a friendly staff that takes our coffee quality seriously, while offering up a wide selection of delectable homemade desserts, fresh deli sandwiches, bagels and soup. We are well known for our fresh hot scones and muffins each morning so come early or call ahead! *Call us for your catering and/or party needs.

Peanut Butter Cup Cookie

½ c. butter
½ c. sugar
½ c. brown sugar
1 large egg
½ tsp. vanilla

1¼ c. flour
¾ tsp. baking soda
½ tsp. salt
2 - 14 oz bags Reese's Mini
    Peanut Butter Cups (or alternate)

Directions

In a large bowl with mixer on high, beat butter, sugars, and peanut butter til smooth, add vanilla and egg til blended. Add flour, soda, and salt - mix on low for 1 minute. Spoon 1 inch mounds of dough into 1½ inch mini muffin pan that measure ¾" deep. (Can line pan with mini paper cups if available for ease of removal from pan) Bake 8-10 minutes at 350˚. Remove papers from peanut butter cups and press into warm cookies, until only the tops show. Cool completely before removing from pan.

*Try alternating your cookie taste by using caramel or fudge cups. Enjoy with a good steamy cup of coffee or cold glass of milk!!

Submitted by Dani Kvern, owner

Mud St. CAFE

In Unique UNDERGROUND Eureka

**Great Food
Espresso
Spirits & more**

Est. 1995

Located at the intersection of
Spring St. and Main St
22 G South Main
Eureka Springs, AR 72632
(479) 254-6732
www.mudstreetcafe.com

We are in what locals call "Underground Eureka." Our building was built in 1888 and at that time we were street level. There is a spring that runs underneath us that in the late 1880s kept flooding the street. Thus the name "Mud Street." The street has since been built up, putting our level down a flight of stairs. We have wonderful old limestone walls, large wooden beams and stained glass lighting.

A favorite for Eureka Springs dining, our food is always fresh and our service is always friendly. We are here to serve you breakfast from 8 a.m. to 11 a.m. and lunch from 11 a.m. to 3 p.m. Closed Wednesdays.

The Mud Street Muffin
The Basic Recipe for 12 Muffins

3½ c. of flour
1 tsp. salt
⅔ c. melted butter
2 eggs (at room temperature or
place in hot water for 5 minutes)

1 c. sugar
1½ tsp. baking soda
1¾ c. buttermilk (microwave
for 40 seconds)
1 tsp. vanilla

Crumb Mixture

1⅓ c. of flour
½ c. brown sugar (heaping)

½ c. white sugar (heaping)
½ c. softened butter

Mix ingredients together in food processor until mixed together giving the consistency of bread crumbs

Directions

Grease two muffin top pans with pan spray. Measure and sift dry ingredients together into large bowl. Make well in center and add half of the buttermilk and the melted butter. Add the two eggs and the vanilla to the remaining buttermilk and beat well with a fork, then add to the other ingredients.

Mix until all of the dry ingredients have just been incorporated into the liquid, but being careful not to over mix. Divide batter evenly between the twelve muffin cups. Top each with approximately 1 Tbsp. of the crumb mixture. Bake at 360° for 17 minutes.

To test for doneness tap top gently with finger. If it feels solid they are done. If it is soft then continue baking for 2 minutes more and test again. Different flavors require different baking times.

Submitted by Bobbie Foster, owner

NEIGHBOR'S MILL BAKERY & CAFE

1012 Hwy. 62-65 North
Harrison, AR 72601
(870) 741-6455
www.neighborsmill.com
email: neighborsmill@alltel.net

At Neighbor's Mill Bakery & Café bread is the star of the show as we handcraft over 25 varieties. (You can see all of them on our website: neighborsmill.com). We sell our breads in our bakery and to grocery stores and health food stores throughout the region. We also use our breads in our café to produce unforgettable grilled and cold sandwiches and we serve them with our soups and signature salads. Our building is a historical reconstruction of an old grist mill. We even use a 100+ year-old mill to grind our chemical free whole grains daily.

The Governor's Muffin
Governor Huckabee's
BANANA-ORANGE MUFFINS

9 c. rolled oats
2 c. firmly packed brown sugar
1 Tbsp. baking soda
1½ tsp. salt
4½ c. buttermilk
6 large eggs, lightly beaten
¾ c. peanut oil

6 c. all-purpose flour
2 Tbsp. baking powder
1 Tbsp. ground cinnamon
2 c. chopped raisins (or dates)
4½ c. mashed ripe banana
   (about 12 medium)
3 Tbsp. grated orange peel

Directions

Heat oven to 350° F. Spray 2 muffin tins with pan release. In large bowl, combine oats, flour, brown sugar, baking powder, baking soda, cinnamon, salt and raisins; mix well. In medium bowl, combine buttermilk, banana, egg whites, oil and orange peel; blend well. Add to dry ingredients all at once; stir just until moistened (Do not overmix!)

Fill muffin cups almost full. Bake 30 - 32 minutes or until golden brown. Cool muffins in pan on wire rack 5 minutes; remove from pan. Makes 24 muffins.

Submitted by Dawn Cook, Governor Huckabee's Office

OZARK MOUNTAIN SMOKE HOUSE

Farmington, AR 72730
(800) 643-3437

In 1946 a small smokehouse was built by Roy Sharp and the Ozark Mountain Smoke House was launched as a business/hobby(?). In 1962 Roy's son, Frank, and his wife, Sara, became actively involved in the business, which they still operate (with their four children) on the Sharp farm on the slopes of Mount Kessler. Visitors are cordially invited to visit Mount Kessler and the smokehouse and kitchens of the Ozark Mountain Family.

Molasses Bars

2 c. flour
2 tsp. baking powder
½ c. melted shortening
½ c. molasses
½ c. sugar
1 egg, beaten slightly
½ tsp. cinnamon

¼ tsp. ginger
¼ tsp. salt
1 c. raisins, plumped
½ tsp. baking soda dissolved
  in tsp. hot water
½ c. buttermilk

Directions

Plump raisins in hot water and drain thoroughly. Sift together flour, baking powder, spices and salt. Combine dissolved soda, shortening, molasses, sugar and egg. Add dry ingredients, buttermilk and raisins to shortening mixture. Pour batter ½" deep in greased pan, 13x9x2". Sprinkle generously with sugar and bake at 350° for 25 to 30 minutes.

Black Walnut Pralines

10 c. sugar
1 lb. brown sugar
2 c. black walnut meats
3 c. sorghum

1 qt. water
12-oz. can evaporated milk
2 Tbsp. vinegar
½ tsp. salt

Directions

Mix all ingredients and cook to 238° F. stirring occasionally. Take from the fire and add ¼ lb. butter (let it float on top). Let cool to 190° F. Stir until candy thickens and drop into patties on greased surfaced. This recipe makes 75, 2 to 3-oz. pralines. If the candy hardens too quickly before all the pralines are formed, the batch may be reheated until it is soft enough to pour.

Submitted by Ozark Mountain Family Cookbook

10 Skywatch
Walnut Ridge, AR 72476
(870) 886-5918

The Parachute Inn, located at the Walnut Ridge Regional Airport, is famous not only for their delicious food and superior service, but also for the atmosphere of dining on a retired Boeing 737 Jet, a truly unique experience. The Parachute Inn has been open for five years, and in that time has welcomed guests from 48 states and foreign countries around the world. Come and join everyone at the Parachute Inn, great food and a wonderful experience is guaranteed!

Quick Peach Cobbler

Serve warm with ice cream.

1 c. self-rising flour
1 c. sugar
1 large can sweetened peaches

1 c. milk
1½ sticks butter
Sprinkle of cinnamon

Directions

In baking dish, melt 1½ sticks of butter. Mix flour, sugar, and milk. Pour batter into baking dish. Pour peaches over batter and sprinkle with cinnamon. Bake at 350°F for 45 minutes or until crust is golden brown.

Submitted by Donna Robertson, owner

RED APPLE INN
AND COUNTRY CLUB

1000 Country Club Road
Heber Springs, AR 72543
1-800-RED-APPLE
www.redappleinn.com

The Red Apple Inn Resort is located in the foothills of the Ozark Mountains on beautiful Greer's Ferry Lake. We offer fine dining with an assortment of steaks, seafood, and homemade dessert in our dining room overlooking the lake. The Inn was designed by a student of Frank Lloyd Wright and blends in with the natural surroundings of Eden Isle.

The Red Apple Inn Icky Sticky Date Dessert

14 oz. brown sugar
8 oz. cream
1 tsp. soda
2 oz. butter, melted
1 tsp. vanilla
7 oz. flour

8 oz. butter
6 oz. dates
10 oz. boiling water
3½ oz. brown sugar
1 egg
1½ tsp. baking powder

Directions

Boil first three ingredients together for 5 minutes or until it starts to brown and thicken slightly. Pour half of sauce into springform pan lined with buttered foil. Reserve rest of sauce. Heat oven to 350°. Pit dates and place in bowl of soda. Pour hot water over and allow to cool. Combine butter, extra sugar and vanilla and beat until the mixture is creamed. Add egg and stir in the date mixture. Mix together the flour and baking powder and fold through until everything is incorporated. Pour into lined pan and bake for 30 minutes. then decrease temp to 315° for another 60 minutes. Serve hot with reserved butterscotch sauce. May also be made in a greased souffle dish or individual bundt pans (greased). Just cut back the cooking time.

Submitted by David Smith

RiverSide Kitchen

2 Frost Street
Gilbert, AR 72636
(870) 439-2288

Next to the Buffalo River and the small town of Gilbert, AR is where you will find the Award Winning RiverSide Kitchen, where anyone who comes in, is a stranger for a minute, and family from then on. With foods made from scratch...huge yeast rolls, decadent fudge cake, bread pudding and fresh baked cinnamon rolls...to an almost endless variety of main entrees from fried catfish with real mashed potatoes and gravy, smoked meats, Mexican food, full pound burger or a juicy ribeye. RiverSide is a regular stop for those traveling to and from Eureka Springs and Branson and now does catering for private and corporate events.

I Can't Believe It's a Cookie!
We make these easy and hard to believe moist cookies as a dessert for our kids meals...there is no flour in this cookie!

2 c. peanut butter
2 eggs

2 c. sugar
2 tsp. vanilla extract

Directions

Mix all ingredients until blended (mixture will be soft). Roll into balls the size of large marbles, or bigger if you want a bigger cookie. Place on an ungreased cookie sheet about 1 inch apart. Press down with a fork dipped in sugar in a crisscross pattern, then bake in 350° oven for about 12 minutes. Do not over bake!

Submitted by Jill Hackett, owner

RUBY'S PLACE

We Guarantee Fast Service
No Matter How Long It Takes!

300 Hwy. 43 East
Harrison, AR 72601
(870) 741-8166

Home of the Nacho Salad and Pepsi Slush. Our motto is we guarantee fast service no matter how long it takes. We feature homemade daily specials. We also have sandwiches, burgers, hot dogs, nachos and pasta salad.

Melt in Your Mouth Cheesecake

1 - 8 oz. pkg. cream cheese
1 - 3 oz. lemon Jello
1 can evaporated milk (chilled)

1 c. sugar
1 c. hot water
Graham cracker crust

Directions

In a large bowl cream together the cream cheese and sugar. In another bowl dissolve the Jello in the hot water. Mix these together. Beat the milk until it forms stiff peaks. Fold the cream cheese mixture into the milk. Pour into a 9" x 13" pan with Graham cracker crust. Chill overnight.

Submitted by Ruby Clayborn

We're Proud to Serve You!

Through 5 generations of Colemans...serving your family is not just a job to us...it's our HERITAGE!

SODIE'S FOUNTAIN & GRILL

Flippin Depot
Junction US Hwy 62/412 and AR Hwy 178
109 N. First Street
Flippin, Arkansas 72634
(870) 453-7632
www.sodies.com

Sodie's Fountain & Grill is located in a recreated turn of the century train station. Complete with antique soda fountain, mirrored back bar, and 20-foot marble counter, Sodie's will take you back to a time when the corner drug store was the town's gathering place. Sodie's serves an extensive, homemade, breakfast, lunch and dinner menu, along with all your favorite ice cream treats. There is also a big gift shop, patio seating, and meeting room. Bus and RV parking is available in the rear of the building. Sodie's is open daily except Thanksgiving, Christmas and New Year's.

Old Fashioned Ice Cream Soda

In a soda glass, or large drink glass, mix 2 oz. of flavored syrup with 1 oz. of vanilla ice cream. Add 2 oz. of carbonated water, mix well. Add one scoop (3 oz.) vanilla ice cream. Fill glass with carbonated water and stir lightly. Top with whipped cream. Enjoy!

Submitted by Gary & Maureen Fancher

SPAVINAW SUPPER CLUB

11662 N. Highway 59
Gravette, AR 72736
(479) 787-7300

This restaurant is located in a traditional century-old Ozark farmhouse that has been restored. It is surrounded by a 700-acre ranch divided by Spavinaw Creek, which is fed upstream by natural springs. There is no entertainment at the club, just gracious dining in the three dining rooms or, when weather permits, on a deck overlooking the stream. Dinner only is served Tuesday through Saturday from 5 p.m. to 10 p.m.

Reservations suggested. Closed Mondays and the month of January. The club is owned and operated by John and Janice Lykins. It is located 2 miles south of Gravette on State Highway 59 South.

Pene's Cheesecake

1½ lbs. cream cheese	1 c. sugar
Juice of 1 lemon	3 eggs
1 tsp. vanilla	Crust (see recipe below)
Topping (see recipe below)	

Directions

Soften cream cheese at room temperature or in microwave. In a blender combine sugar, lemon juice, eggs and vanilla. Process until well blended. Slowly add cream cheese a quarter-pound at a time, blending until smooth after each addition. Pour into crust-lined 10" spring form pan and bake at 375° for 20 minutes. Do not overbake, filling will be soft. When cake is baked remove from oven, increase temperature to 500°. Gently spoon topping evenly over cake. Return to oven and bake for 5 minutes at 500°. Refrigerate overnight before serving. Makes 6 portions.

Crust: Thoroughly mix 1¼ c. Graham cracker crumbs, 2 Tbsp. sugar, 1½ tsp. cinnamon and 6 Tbsp. melted butter. Pat mixture onto the bottom only of a 10" spring form pan.

Topping : Combine 12 oz. sour cream (needs to be at room temperature), 3 Tbsp. sugar and 1 tsp. vanilla and stir until smooth.

Submitted by Nancy Kennedy

SPICE O'LIFE BAKERY/CAFE

"The Natural Tastes of Arkansas"
200 N. Spring St.
Jasper, AR 72641
(870) 446-2468

Since 1993 we have lived up to our byline, "The Natural Taste of Arkansas," by using locally grown produce and even naturally occurring fruits and berries as available. We serve deli-style lunch Tuesday through Friday and pizza and pasta on Friday and Saturday nights. We make pastries and special occasion cakes. We also bake bread and cookies for both retail and wholesale markets.

Cherry Cheese Pie

9" Graham cracker crust
1 c. powdered sugar
1 c. Cool Whip

1 - 8 oz. pkg. cream cheese, softened
½ tsp. vanilla
1 can cherry pie filling

Directions

Mix softened cream cheese, powdered sugar, vanilla and Cool Whip. Place in bottom of crust. Spoon pie filling over top. Chill. Decorate with more Cool Whip if desired.

Paw Paw Muffins

2 c. paw paw pulp
1½ c. (3 sticks) margarine
6 eggs
6 c. all-purpose flour
½ tsp. salt

1 tsp. lemon juice
1¾ c. sugar
1 tsp. lemon extract
1 Tbsp. baking powder
½ tsp. nutmeg

Directions

Mix paw paw pulp with lemon juice and set aside. Cream margarine and sugar. Add eggs, beating until smooth. Add paw paw pulp and lemon extract and beat until smooth. Mix flour, baking powder, salt and nutmeg. Add alternately with milk. Spoon into greased or lined large muffin tins. Bake at 375° for 20-22 minutes. Makes approximately 2 dozen large size muffins.

Submitted by Leon and Jan Doud, owners

SPRING ST. GRILL

101 N. Spring
Springdale, AR 72764
(479) 751-0323

This is a simple recipe and perhaps the beauty is in its simplicity. It came from my mother who was the real influence behind my cooking and baking career. Probably just sentiment, but it has always been my favorite pumpkin pie.

Babe's Pumpkin Pie

3 eggs
1 c. Libby pumpkin
1 tsp. nutmeg
½ tsp. salt

⅔ c. sugar
1½ c. milk
1 tsp. cinnamon

Directions

Lightly scaled milk and set aside. On low speed mixer combine all ingredients then add warm milk. Pour into unbaked 9" pie crust and bake at 450° for 10-15 minutes. Reduce heat to 350° and continue baking for 30-35 minutes or until knife inserted into center comes out clean.

Submitted by Bill Palkowsky

540 Sidney St.
St. James, MO 65559
(800) 280-9463
www.StJamesWinery.com

St. James Winery is owned and operated by the Hofherr Family since 1970, conveniently located on Interstate 44, on Old Historic Route 66 only ninety miles southwest of St. Louis, Missouri in St. James, Missouri .

With over 700 miles of vines in Missouri, Arkansas, and Michigan, no other winery in the Eastern United states utilizes such state of the art technology from the vineyards to the bottling room bringing you consistent quality vintages for your enjoyment. With over 1,800 medals to date, no wonder St. James Winery is "America's Midwest Winery". In our area, be sure to stop by our tasting room and sample our wide variety of vintages, our extensive gift shop, and take a tour of our cellars. St. James Winery products are presently distributed in six states and available on our website.

Elegant Pears with Red Wine Glaze

½ c. St. James Winery Friendship School Red Wine
2 - 15 oz. cans pear halves, packed in their own juice (not heavy syrup)
1 c. sugar
Ground cinnamon

Juice from 1/2 lemon
Fresh mint for garnish

Directions

Drain juice from pears. Discard juice or reserve for another use. Divide pears evenly, center side up, into four shallow dessert bowls. Set aside.

Combine sugar, wine and lemon juice in a two quart sauce pan. Place over medium heat, stirring constantly. Bring mixture to a boil. Continue stirring and cook mixture until it thickens, about 2 minutes. Immediately remove from heat.

Drizzle syrup evenly over pears, pooling syrup in the cored center of the fruit. Dust lightly with cinnamon. Garnish with fresh mint. Serve at once.

Submitted by Jack Bonar

SUGAR MOUNTAIN

2396 N. College Ave
Fayetteville AR 72703
(479) 443-9500
sugarmtnroadhouse@yahoo.com

Sugar Mountain Roadhouse was originally established as a restaurant and gallery in which the owners featured some local artists work as well as some well known prints for sale. In September of 2005, changes were made, in management, food and atmosphere. Changes continued to present day July, 2006. The restaurant and gallery has now become a roadhouse bar and refined dining establishment. As a local journalist described, "rough and refined", (Arkansas Democrat Gazette, June 2006).

The restaurant/soda fountain serves Burgers, Barbeque and Steaks as well as a full array of fountain treats. The bar features nightly drink specials, Texas Hold'em Poker and Karaoke two nights a week. Sugar Mountain Roadhouse is a fun place to go for a nice dinner or just plain ol' fun at the bar. Located in Fayetteville, Arkansas on the corner of Township and College (71B), you can't miss it. So whenever you are in the area, drop on in, we will be glad to serve you some really good barbeque and fun.

Sweet Potato Pie – Straight from the South

Prepare and set aside one 10 pastry crust.
Set out 1½ c. sweet potatoes or yams-mashed.
Scald 1½ c. milk–in double boiler, heat milk over water until a skim forms on top.

Combine :

2 Tbsp. butter	½ c. firmly packed brown sugar
1 tsp. cinnamon	½ tsp. ginger
¼ tsp. mace	¼ tsp. salt

Directions

Mix with sweet potatoes and add 2 well beaten eggs. Blend with scalded milk and turn into pastry shell. Bake at 450° for 10 minutes. Reduce heat to 350° and bake 35-40 minutes longer or until metal knife inserted halfway between center and edge comes out clean.

Cool and serve with whip cream.

Submitted by Tina St. John-Horner, manager

Gourmet Espresso Bar

412 W. Dickson St.
Fayetteville, AR
(479) 442-3515
www.commongroundsar.com

Common Grounds is dedicated to keeping the "Coffee Craze" alive in Fayetteville. Common Grounds boasts a lively atmosphere and diverse nature in their establishment, a true reflection of the Dickson Street neighborhood. They are proud to serve the best quality and widest variety of coffee drinks in town. You will find the atmosphere at Common Grounds draws you in for a muffin and a morning cup of Joe, a salad and your favorite sandwich for lunch, and even an after-dinner drink over light conversation with your friends.

Espresso Cheesecake

Crust:
   6 c. Oreo crumbs   1½ sticks butter

Batter:
   12 oz. chocolate chips`   64 oz. cream cheese
   1⅓ c. sugar   6 large eggs
   ⅔ c. milk   4 shots expresso

Glaze:
   1 c. chocolate chips   6 Tbsp. butter
   1 Tbsp. + 1 tsp. corn syrup

Directions

Preheat convection oven to 300 degrees. Spray two spring form pans with pan spray. Combine butter and Oreo crumbs. Press crumb mixture into bottom of pans to form crust. Bake 4 minutes at 300˚.

In mixer, combine cream cheese, sugar, melted chocolate, eggs, milk and espresso until smooth. Pour batter mixture into crusts. Bake for 35-40 minutes. Remove from oven. Once cool, decorate with glaze.

Yield: 2 cakes

Submitted by Kari Larson and Julie Sill, co-owners

THE FEED STORE CAFE

THE FEED STORE CAFE
GENTRY, ARKANSAS

136 S. Gentry Blvd.
Gentry, AR 72734
(479) 736-3481

The Feed Store Cafe is located in Gentry, AR. It is owned by Herb and Pat Varner. It has been owned, operated and in the same location for almost 12 years. The Feed Store Cafe has excellent homemade food, friendly staff and wonderful small town charm. Y'all come and see us!

Better Than Almost Anything Cake

1 German chocolate cake mix
1 jar caramel ice cream topping
1 bag of Heath Bar toffee and
  chocolate bits

1 can sweetened condensed milk
1 med. to large bowl of Cool Whip
  depending on how much you like

Directions

Bake cake as directed and when done and still hot, poke holes in top of cake and pour sweetened condensed milk on top. Let sit for 15 to 20 minutes while milk absorbs into cake. Pour caramel topping over cake and refrigerate at least one hour. The longer it refrigerates the better it is. Top with Cool Whip and sprinkle Heath Bar bits on top of whipped topping.

Submitted by Herb & Pat Varner, owner

THE STATION CAFE

111 N Main St.
Bentonville AR 72712
(479) 273-0553

The Station Cafe Inc. was established in 1997. It is a homestyle family restaurant with an extensive menu to please everyone's palate. Best known for our Black Angus Steakburgers, we also have weekly specials that range from chicken kabobs to stuffed cabbages. Voted in Reader Choice Awards - 2005 as Best Burger, Best Freedom Fry, Best Place to Eat Lunch. Your satisfaction is guaranteed at The Station Cafe Inc. We proudly serve Edy's Grand Ice Cream.

Cake Icing

1 stick butter
3 Tbsp. vanilla
2 Tbsp. chocolate liqueur

¼ can evaporated milk
5 Tbsp. cocoa powder
2 boxes powdered sugar

Directions

Melt butter and place in mixer. Then add evaporated milk, vanilla, cocoa powder, chocolate liqueur and mix well. Add powdered sugar slowly, mix until smooth. This recipe will ice up to 3 cakes. Store in refrigerator with lid. Will keep 2 weeks or longer. Add water if too stiff.

Submitted by Cecil Turner, owner

TOOTHPICKS CHOPHOUSE

324 W. Dickson St.
Fayetteville, AR 72701
(479) 521-6880

At Toothpicks we sell the finest meat money can buy and age the beef for 50 days before we serve it. We also slow smoke our BBQ meats for at least 12 hours with a dry rub. Here is our best selling dessert for your enjoyment.

Drop Cobbler

1½ c. flour
2½ tsp. baking powder
¼ c. melted butter
¼ c. sugar for sweet fruit

1½ c. sugar
1 c. milk
15 oz. fruit filling (choose your favorite)
½ c. sugar for tart fruit

Directions

This is the easiest cobbler in the world. All you do is mix the flour, sugar, baking powder, milk and butter. Pour into small baking dish, then put fruit on top of it and cook at 350° for 20 minutes.

Submitted by chef Tim Freeman

VILLAGE WHEEL RESTAURANT

1400 Central Blvd.
Bull Shoals, AR 72619
(870) 445-4414

The Village Wheel Restaurant, located in beautiful Bull Shoals, AR has been family-owned for 24 years, serving breakfast, lunch and dinner 7 days a week. Owners Cindy Crosslin and Danette Stubenfoll opened a gift shop in March 2005 which has unique gifts for that hard-to-buy-for person. The Village Wheel Restaurant specializes in Broasted Chicken. Monday nights is all you can eat chicken. Wednesday nights feature Canadian Walleye, Thursday nights feature quail, Friday nights has all you can eat popcorn shrimp or Alaskan white fish and Saturday nights offer prime rib. Skillet breakfasts have also been added to the menu. There is a private dining room for banquets and regular customers enjoy our birthday and anniversary club.

Carrot Puff

1 lb. carrots, peeled and cut in 1" pieces
3 eggs
3 Tbsp. flour
1 tsp. vanilla

½ c. margarine, melted
1 c. granulated sugar
1 tsp. baking powder

Directions

Preheat oven to 350°. Grease an 8-inch square baking dish. Place carrots in a medium size saucepan and cover with salted water. Bring to a boil; reduce heat and simmer, uncovered for 20 minutes or until carrots are tender. Drain. Place margarine, eggs, sugar, flour, baking powder and vanilla in food processor or blender. Add carrots and puree the mixture. Pour into prepared baking dish. Bake at 350° for 45 minutes or until firm. Let stand for 5 minutes. Serves 6.

Submitted by Cindy & Danette, owners

702 Highway 56
Calico Rock, AR 72519
(870)297-3999
www.whiterivercafe.com

White River Café, nestled in the foothills of the Ozark Mountains in Calico Rock, Arkansas, caters to a unique local community and the many anglers searching for the perfect trout on the nationally known White River. Established in 1972, and still family owned and operated, the Café is known for its "you catch them we cook them" philosophy. Tourists and locals alike especially enjoy the Café's homemade pies and salads. After a day lounging by the creek or fishing the White River beneath the majestic bluffs, locals and tourists clamor for the Café's "Coconut Crème Pie" or our "Bacon/Ranch Pasta Salad."

White River Cafe Coconut Crème Pie

This Coconut Crème Pie has been made at the Café for over 30 years. Long time employee Louise Stetka puts her magic touch on every pie!

Mix together in large saucepan:

2½ c. sugar

4 heaping Tbsp. cornstarch

6½-7 cups milk (1 cup cold; 5½-6 c. warmed 4 min. in micro)

1 heaping Tbsp. flour

6 slightly beaten egg yolks

Dash of salt

Heat over medium high heat until thick and bubbly
Remove from heat and stir in:

½ c. butter

2 tsp. vanilla

½ bag sweetened coconut

Directions

Pour into pre-baked, cooled pie shells. For meringue: Beat 6 egg whites to stiff meringue, add ½ tsp. crème of tartar, spread over cooled pies. Sprinkle additional coconut over top of meringue. Bake at 350° for 6-8 minutes to brown meringue. Allow to cool completely, then refrigerate for at least one hour before serving. Makes 2 9-inch pies.

Submitted by Louise Stetka

Index

DESSERTS